SCENERY TIPS AND TECHNIQUES

From **Model Railroader** Magazine

MODEL RAILROAD HANDBOOK NO. 26

Cover photo by John Olson
Cover design by Larry Luser

The material in this book first appeared as articles in MODEL RAILROADER Magazine

KALMBACH **BOOKS**

First printing, 1989. Second printing, 1990. Third printing, 1992.

Plaster-gauze scenery

And should you happen to break an arm . . . .

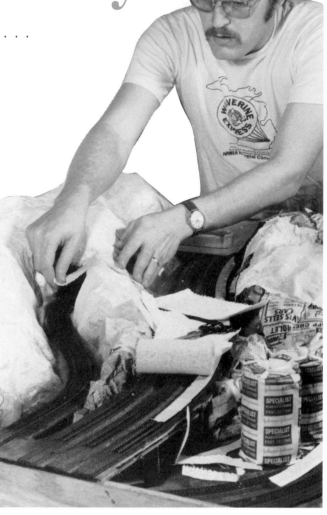

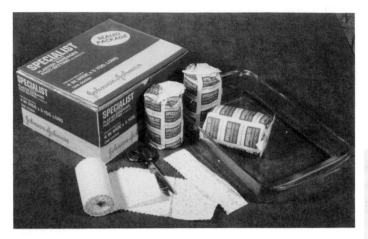

Materials needed for plaster-gauze scenery include gauze, scissors, and a bowl of water. The wet gauze is stiff enough to hold its shape with minimal support.

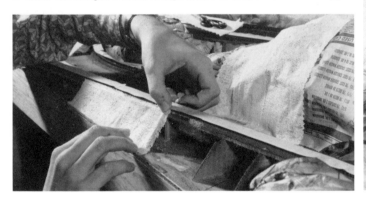

BY GREG JOHNSON

JUST mention the word "scenery" to some model railroaders and they cringe at the thought of gallons of gooey plaster and dripping paper towels fouling their floors and jamming their turnout points. Never fear; there is an alternative. It involves the use of plaster-impregnated gauze, the same stuff the doctor uses to make a cast for junior's broken arm.

The technique has been around for a while, but on the whole it appears to have been a well-kept secret. I first saw it demonstrated several years ago at a local mini-convention; since then I have put the technique to good use on Ntrak modules as well as on my N scale Gulf, Colorado & Santa Fe RR.

The process is simple. The gauze is cut into strips, dipped in water for about 5 seconds, then applied over a base of newspaper, wire, cardboard, or anything that will hold its shape for a few minutes. The great thing about this technique is how clean it is. There is virtually no drip, no oozing mess. Only minimal protection is needed for trackwork and adjacent scenery.

The material, produced by Johnson & Johnson under the trade name "Specialist Bandage," is available at most large medical supply houses. It comes in boxes of 12 individually sealed rolls in 2″, 4″, and 6″ widths. Each roll is 5 yards long. The current price per carton of 12 rolls of 4″ material runs about $16. A 4″ roll will yield about 4 square feet of scenery.

The gauze makes a very good scenery base for all types of topography. Rugged contours are formed over wadded-up newspapers, and rolling hills come from placing gauze over screen wire or large pieces of thin cardboard lattice. The gauze method is especially useful for remodeling or repairing existing scenery. Its slight stiffness and light weight make it hold its shape well, unlike a plaster-soaked paper towel which needs much stouter support.

To begin the gauze application you need a minimum of supplies: rolls of plaster gauze, scissors, spray bottle, Pyrex or plastic bowl, and underlayment (wadded-up newspaper, screen wire or card forms). Spray the underlayment lightly with water so it accepts the wet plaster gauze better and doesn't draw the moisture from it. Cut strips of gauze approximately 8″ to 10″ long plus some smaller sizes for special areas. Immerse the strips, one at a time, for 3 to 5 seconds; then drape them over the under-layment. Allow each succeeding strip to overlap slightly.

To insure a good bond with the adjoining strip, lightly rub the joint with a fingernail so that the plaster from one strip completely "mixes" with the plaster from the other. This also helps to hide the joints.

The gauze sets in about 30 minutes; it should be completely dry in about 3 or 4 hours, depending on humidity. As with other plaster techniques, when adding more gauze to existing plaster gauze scenery, prewetting is necessary.

Gauze is not nearly as strong as Hydrocal, so if the scenery base is to support the weight of many rock castings, additional layers of gauze or a thin coat of brushed-on Hydrocal will be necessary.

The gauze can be finished in many ways. Zip-texturing and water-soluble scenery are two of the best. The latter method (which uses diluted, earth-tone latex paint to affix the ground cover) when combined with the gauze produces very fast and clean scenery.

Don't let the "fear of trying" keep you from attempting some scenery work. With the plaster-gauze method you needn't worry about making a mess. Take that first step and get started on one of the most relaxing facets of model railroading. ✿

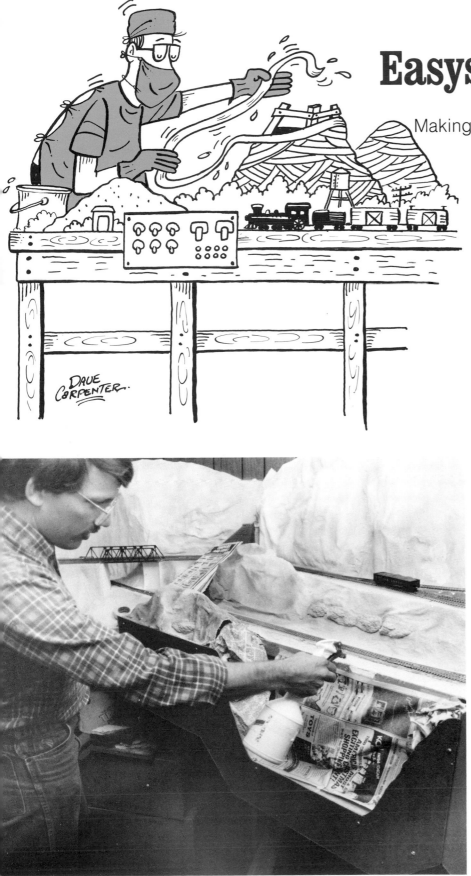

Easyshell scenery

Making hardshell without the mess

BY BRAD SHORT
PHOTOS BY THE AUTHOR

MAKING REALISTIC SCENERY isn't the difficult task many fear. Actually, it is one aspect of our hobby where there are so many variations in the prototype (Mother Nature) that it's hard to be wrong. Yet many model railroaders seem to get stalled when construction reaches the scenery stage. In our desire to get the trains running, we feverishly build the benchwork, lay track, install the wiring — and then stop, as though we needed sand under our wheels.

Every layout has to have benchwork, roadbed, track, structures, and wiring, but what makes layouts memorable is the scenery. Scenery is like the artist's paint on his canvas — it defines the creation, brings it to life.

One of the greatest developments in the model railroading hobby in recent years has been hardshell scenery. Using it you can quickly build a lightweight, self-supporting terrain shell using plaster-soaked paper toweling. However, I found some parts of the process were really *hard*. It was *hard* to find Hydrocal plaster in my area. It was *hard* to mix the plaster to the proper consistency. It was *hard* to build scenery on my layout in a spare bedroom without messing up the house with plaster dust.

Just when I was about to give up on scenery, I read an article on a variation of hardshell scenery using a plaster-impregnated material intended for making casts for setting broken bones. This sounded interesting, so I got some from a friend who's an orthopedic surgeon and gave it a try. It worked great!

All of the problems I'd had with *hard*shell were eliminated. There's no mixing, no waste, no mess — and best of all, it's interruptible. You can work for a short time, stop to take a phone call, empty the trash, watch a football game, and then take up right where you left off. I began calling it *easy*shell.

Later I found that, like many "new" ideas in our hobby, the plaster-mesh scenery technique was tried as long as 30 years ago by members of a local club here in the Kansas City area. Regardless, I think it's a great technique which hasn't received much publicity. If it's "new" for you, follow along and I'll explain how the process works.

PREPARATION

The first step is gathering the necessary materials. Here's what you'll need:

Step 1. Using your spray bottle, wet the newspapers *and* any benchwork or subroadbed surfaces (as Fred Jakobsen is doing in the photo above) to be covered with the plaster-mesh easyshell. It's best to thoroughly wet the wood first so it doesn't draw the water from the plaster-impregnated mesh.

3

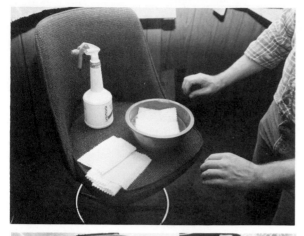

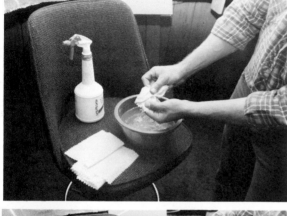

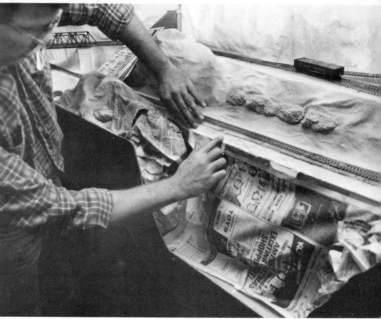

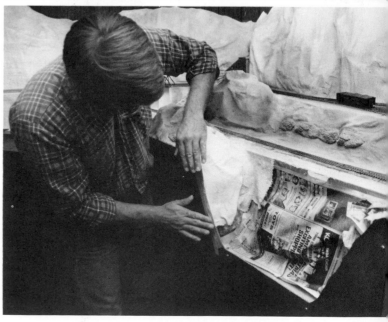

Step 2. Top. Place a strip of plaster mesh into a bowl of very warm water. You want to wet the plaster in the mesh thoroughly without soaking it. This takes only about 5 seconds. If you just drop the pieces in the water and let them soak, some of the plaster washes away and the result is a weaker shell. **Center.** As you pick the strip out of the water, give it a gentle accordian squeeze over the bowl to remove excess water. **Above.** Straighten out the gauze and you're ready to start forming the easyshell scenery.

Step 3. Right, top. Begin by draping the strips over the scenery contour, working from the top down. **Right, center.** It's important to rub the edges of the mesh where it adjoins the subroadbed to make the plaster adhere. **Right.** Be sure to rub the strips along the fascia edge to assure a good bond there also. When you place the second and succeeding strips in place, overlap each piece onto its neighbor by about ½". Then rub the overlapping part of the top piece so the plaster in it blends with the plaster in the piece underneath. This assures a firm bond between the two pieces that is essential to the shell's strength. A wet mesh of strips won't be self supporting until it hardens, which takes only 5 to 10 minutes. So, if you're making a hill, lay strips to form the ridge line first. When the ridge line sets up, make the sides of the hill by hanging strips from the ridge layer — much like hanging wallpaper. Rub the hill side strips where they overlap the ridge layer to ensure a good bond.

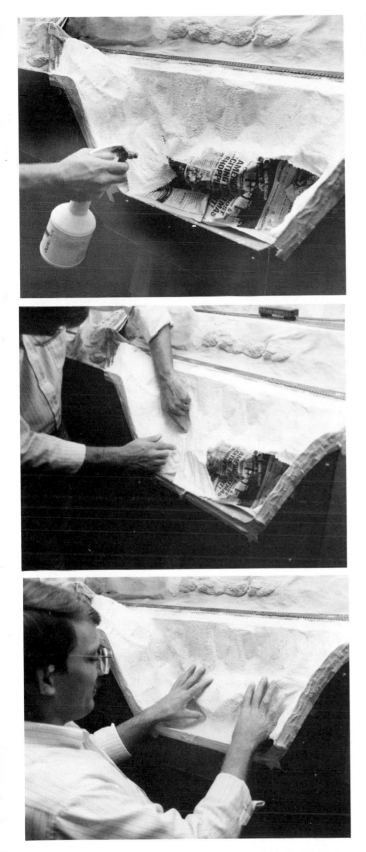

Step 5. After the shell hardens fully (give it a couple of hours), you simply coat it with latex paint of an appropriate earth or rock color. Coating the shell with latex paint does several things. First, it fills any tiny holes in the plaster mesh layers. The paint also protects and toughens the shell while coloring it. Since painting the shell is the first step in the water-soluble texturing process, it is not an extra step, merely the next one. I use a latex sand-texture ceiling paint which I tint to the desired color using a few drops of universal tinting colors sold in paint and hardware stores. A less expensive alternative is to use the cheapest latex paint you can find and add a finely ground "texturing additive" such as Perlite. The succeeding layers of ground foam, real dirt, or other texturing materials, bonded together with matte medium will increase the strength of the easyshell.

● Rolls of plaster mesh material. Several brands are available from medical supply houses, hobby shops, and craft stores. ParisCraft and Rigid Way are two brand names.
● A medium-plastic bowl for wetting the plaster mesh strips.
● A spray bottle filled with water.
● Material to form the basic shell. The cheapest material is old newspapers wadded up to form the base for the shell. Some people prefer to staple together cardboard strips in a basket-weave pattern to form a more controllable contour.
● Masking tape to hold the newspapers in position until you form the shell.

With the materials in hand, the next step is to spread newspapers to protect the floor and anything else that needs protection. Instead of masking tape, I use strips of wetted newspaper to protect the track.

Form the scenery contour using wadded up newspapers or strips of cardboard woven and stapled together.

Cut the plaster mesh into pieces that are 6″ to 8″ in length. I suggest you use a pinking shears. The sides of the plaster mesh material come with a sawtooth edge, and if you make your cuts with a pinking shears all four sides of each piece will have ragged edges, which blend together better when making the shell.

Put about 3″ of very warm water in the plastic bowl. Lukewarm or cool water causes the plaster to set slower; the result is a weaker shell.

At this point you're about ready to begin. Follow the instructions that accompany the photos. Once you find out how simple it is to use plaster mesh to make *easy*shell, there is no good reason for you to stay stalled at the prescenery construction stage. Try sceniking a small area of your layout and you'll find out how easy it is to dramatically change its appearance. ⚙

Step 4. Top. When you add plaster strips to an area where the plaster has hardened, be sure to wet all surfaces where new gauze will be attached. **Center.** Then proceed with the easyshell process until the entire area is covered. **Above.** One thickness of mesh is really pretty fragile, although it will be self supporting. If you don't want eggshell scenery, it's best to go back and add two or three more layers of mesh for additional strength. When you've finished with a scenery-building session, just rinse out the bowl and you're done! There is no other cleanup required. It's recommended that you store any partially used rolls of mesh in a plastic bag.

Rubber rocks, wire weeds, and other scenery tips

These good-looking rocks will bend, but not break

Fig 1. Making sponge rubber rocks.
Start with a piece of sponge . . . .

Spread the caulking around . . . .

BY BERNARD HUGHES
PHOTOS BY THE AUTHOR

I WANTED a new way of making scenery, a quick method that left little mess. I wanted rocks that would bend and not break, yet look realistic. As you can see, all I wanted was miracle scenery.

It took me a full week to think this problem through. Finally it occurred to

Fig. 2. Attaching rocks to the layout.
Apply silicone cement to backing material . . .

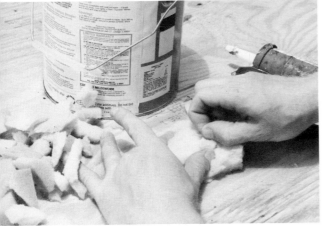

Score with a knife and tear out bits and pieces . . . .

Apply latex caulking . . . .

Paint with latex paint. . . .

Sprinkled on sand adds texture.

me that the only flexible thing around my house was a large, thick piece of sponge foam used for packing. Well, this became the basis of the idea. Then it all came together — my miracle rubber rock scenery!

BASIC ROCK CONSTRUCTION

Sponge rubber is used to make pillows, stuffed toys, what have you, so you can usually find it at variety stores, fabric stores, or upholstery shops. Figure 1 shows the basic steps involved in making rubber rocks.

Starting with a large piece of sponge, tear it into smaller shapes. You don't have to worry about cutting the foam to exact shapes. It will surprise you how it all fits together like a jigsaw puzzle when you cement the rocks to the layout.

To shape an individual piece make

some cuts across it, then pick and tear out bits and pieces.

I use acrylic latex caulking to seal the rock faces. It's inexpensive and remains flexible. You can buy it in many colors, and it takes paint very well — you can even paint it while it's still wet.

I use a caulking gun to apply large amounts of caulking to the foam, then spread it with a butter knife or even my

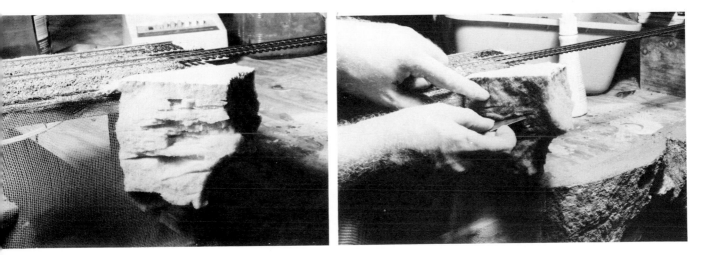

Press rock in place. . . .

Modifications are easy.

finger, making sure to work it into the cracks between pieces to help bond them together. You can wash the caulking off your hands and tools with plain water.

For hard-looking rocks just add more caulking. You can also thin the caulking with water or paint to create a washed-out look. Sprinkling sand on rocks will give them a rough texture.

ADDING THE ROCKS TO THE LAYOUT

You can make rocks one at a time at the workbench, as shown in fig. 1, or you can work with the pieces of sponge in place on the layout.

Any kind of backing will do to support the rocks: wood, cardboard, Styrofoam, or screen wire, just to name a few. I recommend a silicone-based glue for attaching the sponge to the backing — the black variety has worked well for me. As shown in fig. 2, only a small amount is needed to hold the sponge in place.

A nail shoved through the rock will hold it temporarily in position while the glue is drying. After a few minutes you can begin cutting and tearing the sponge to create cracks and crevices. Remember, it's impossible to make a mistake. After all, rocks in nature have no uniform design, so use your imagination. If you're not happy with a particular rock, alterations are easy, using a razor blade or hobby knife.

COLORING THE ROCKS

If you have not used an appropriately colored acrylic latex caulking you will need to apply a base color. I use exterior flat acrylic latex house paint. When buying such paint be sure to check out the table of offshade paints (someone mixed the wrong colors) in the paint store. I have found just the right color at half the price.

Again, you can create washout effects by spraying the paint with water. Sand sprinkled on at this stage will be held by the paint and also colored by it. Also again, the acrylic latex paint will clean up with just soap and water.

I usually wait 24 hours and let the base coat dry to a flat finish, although if I'm in a hurry I will use a hair dryer to speed up the drying time.

Next, I add a lot of different colors to give depth to the rocks. Reds, beiges, grays, golds, and browns are all good. I blend these colors as I go along, then let them dry for a day also. Baby food jars

Fig. 3. Leftover sponge is chopped up and dyed in a blender to make ground foam. Here the dye is being poured off through screen wire. The dye is saved and used to color more of the foam.

are great for mixing paint as you go along. They're easy to hold in your hand, seal well, and open easily.

The next day I add highlights by drybrushing on lighter colors that have been thinned. I let this dry to a flat finish before going on with my scenery.

GROUND COVER

Remember all those little chunks of sponge left over from making rocks? I use mine to make my own ground cover material. I put them in the blender, as shown in fig. 3. Then I add a mixture of half water and half green acrylic paint. I turn the blender on low until all the sponge is covered with paint; then I turn it on high to crumble the sponge into tiny bits.

After a few minutes I turn off the blender and pour the mixture through screen wire to separate the small pieces of foam from the dye. The dye can be used over and over again. I add more acrylic paint to the dye, such as different shades of greens, grays, and browns to create a variety of ground foam.

Next, I remove the foam from the screen wire, pull it apart, and place it in a large bowl to dry.

TWIGS AND SUCH

While waiting for that ground foam to dry, we can begin adding small twigs, rocks, and sand to the bottom and tops of the hillsides for texture. I use white glue to cement my twigs and rocks in place.

Next, I sprinkle sand and ground foam on the flat parts of my scenery. It's a good idea to use more than one shade and size — variety adds life.

I fasten down all these materials by spraying them with diluted white glue. You need to find a spray bottle that will spray a fine mist — a hair-spray bottle works well. Fill the spray bottle with about two thirds water, one third white glue, and a squirt of dishwashing detergent. Spray lightly over the area at first to make the glue flow into the textured material. Be sure to go over the area several times until it is saturated. This process will bond everything together.

TREES AND WEEDS

Most of the trees on my layout came from a chinaberry tree which has limbs of small leafy branches. I remove the leaves outdoors and take the twigs to the workbench where I add ground foam.

Lots of different kinds of weeds can also be used for trees. Be sure to make different heights and various colors of trees for your layout. You may even want to add a little paint to the tips of the foliage to give depth.

To mount trees to the sponge mountain, I first poke a small hole about ½" deep into the foam. I leave the nail in until I'm ready to plant the tree so I won't lose the hole. Again, I use white glue.

You don't need a hole all the way through the foam and into the backing to support the trees. The trees will hold just fine in the foam itself. In fact, if you do mount the trees into the backing, they'll be much more likely to break off if bumped. Mounted in the foam, the trees will bounce back and not break.

I use two different ways of making weeds. One is with stranded wire, as shown in fig. 4.

My other way of making tall grass and weeds is to cut rug twine into about ¼" pieces. For twine weeds I don't punch a hole in the foam, I just glue the twine to the surface of the layout. When painting the twine I thin the paint so it will keep the twine from sticking together in big clumps.

IN CONCLUSION

Let's take one last look at the advantages of rubber rock scenery. You never have to hurry like you do with plaster, so you can be more creative. If you don't like the results, you can just pinch off more sponge or glue some more on. There is no waste — the small pieces of sponge go into the blender to make ground foam.

You'll really appreciate this scenery if you ever have to move the layout. The inevitable knocks and bumps will do no harm, and you'll have the layout up again and running in no time. ✿

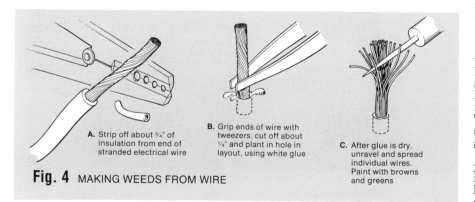

A. Strip off about ¾" of insulation from end of stranded electrical wire

B. Grip ends of wire with tweezers, cut off about ¼" and plant in hole in layout, using white glue

C. After glue is dry, unravel and spread individual wires. Paint with browns and greens

Fig. 4 MAKING WEEDS FROM WIRE

Casting rock walls—Bohemian style

I got the idea while watching my wife make my favorite dessert

BY BOB KUCHAR

PROGRESS on my O scale Lake Forest & Western RR. had progressed through the trackwork stage to the scenery stage. My friends had convinced me of the fantastic beauty and realism of rock castings to the point that I had to use them, or at least something equivalent. Nothing else would suffice. Unfortunately, as the railroad's chief executive, I foresaw problems.

The LF&W is built on a 30"-wide shelf mounted around the periphery of my basement. That would mean a lot of cast rocks. Commercially available castings would look nice but would cost a fortune.

My shelf layout would also mean a lot of tight squeezes where the rocks would have to be ¾" or less thick. For example, I would need a sheer 90-degree vertical rock wall 7" high by at least 15'-0" long and no more than ¾" thick.

Besides these problems, my attempts at making silicone rubber molds had been disastrous. The process is slow and tedious, and the results had been less than acceptable.

I didn't know what to do, so I exercised my executive privilege and shelved the rock wall idea.

A few days later I watched my wife making my favorite dessert, Bohemian coffee cake. She didn't have the correct-size pan, so she improvised, and fashioned a pan from aluminum foil. Lo and behold, her pan was about the thickness and width needed for my rock wall. Again exercising my executive privilege,

Fig. 1. "Bohemian-style" rock castings begin with a wooden 1 x 2 frame nailed to a flat surface, such as a workbench. The rocky texture is created by the addition of wadded newspaper.

Fig. 2. Next, crinkled aluminum foil is worked down into the frame, over the wads of paper.

Fig. 3. After the foil is sprayed with a silicone lubricant, plaster is poured into the mold.

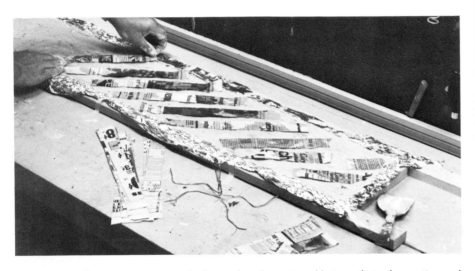

Fig. 4. Strips of newspaper are worked into the plaster to add strength to the casting and to cover any islands of foil that may protrude. Six or seven layers of paper are needed.

Fig. 5. Loops of wire inserted into the wet plaster must be secured with several layers of paper-plaster strips. The loops will be secured to the benchwork to hold the casting in place.

Fig. 6. The finished casting looks like this before it is removed from the mold. To remove it, pull the mold frame apart. Trying to pull the casting from the frame could result in breakage.

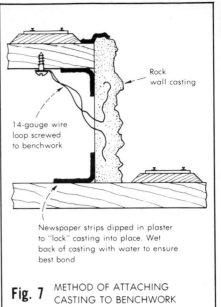

Rock wall casting

14-gauge wire loop screwed to benchwork

Newspaper strips dipped in plaster to "lock" casting into place. Wet back of casting with water to ensure best bond

Fig. 7 METHOD OF ATTACHING CASTING TO BENCHWORK

I confiscated her roll of foil and her favorite mixing bowl and dived into the depths of the basement. Out of my efforts the following procedure for making rock walls evolved.

Forming, filling the mold

Tack a frame of 1 x 2 lumber to a flat surface, such as the top of a workbench. My frame measured 7″ wide (the height needed for my wall), ¾″ deep, and 3′-1″ to 4′-0″ long. Roll up about a dozen wads of newspaper and drop them into the frame. See fig. 1. They help ensure that the rock wall will have a rugged texture, not like the flat bottom of a Bohemian coffee cake.

Unroll 4 to 5 feet of foil and crinkle it into a ball. Then unroll the ball carefully, so as not to tear the foil. Work it down into the frame, over the wads of paper: fig. 2. It may help to hold the foil edges to the frame with masking tape. After the general shape looks good, spray the inside of the mold with an aerosol silicone lubricant* to prevent the foil from sticking to the rock casting.

Prepare a batch of Hydrocal, patching plaster, or plaster of paris, and pour it into the mold: fig. 3. When the mold is filled, work strips of newspaper down into the plaster. See fig. 4. This is an important step to add strength, so that the wall won't fall apart before it is mounted on the layout, and to cover any islands of foil that may protrude above the surface of the plaster. Six or seven layers of paper, each laid in a different pattern, works fine.

At this time, add a few loops of 14-gauge bare copper wire: fig. 5. The loops will be screwed to the railroad benchwork to hold the wall section in place. Cover the tails of each loop with several layers of paper to make sure they don't pull out when the plaster has hardened. Plan the location of the loops so that they will be in a convenient position for mounting on the benchwork.

When the plaster has hardened, pull

*Slide Silicone Mold Release, Percy Harms Corp., Skokie, Ill.—or any other silicone spray will do. I've also heard that a dull-finish aerosol spray such as Floquil or Testors Dullcote works well.

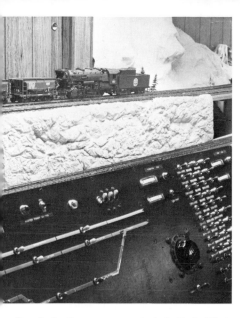

Fig. 8. Sections are mounted, butted, filled.

the mold frame apart to free the casting. If the casting is pulled directly out of the frame, it is likely to crack; thus, it's safer to break the frame apart. Peel off and discard the foil.

If the casting looks like a plaster copy of crinkled aluminum foil and not real rocks, don't fret. Also, don't worry about air bubbles. They will be eliminated later. For now, mount the wall on the railroad.

Mounting, finishing touches

Hopefully the wire loops will be in a strategic location. Pull them taut and mount them on the railroad with wood screws. To help lock the wall permanently to the layout, build the corners up with strips of paper dipped into plaster. See fig. 7. It's a good idea to wet the plaster down: liberally brush on coats of water. This will aid the newspaper-plaster strips to adhere.

If this first casting looks good, calculate the quantity and lengths of the remaining sections to complete the wall. When all sections have been mounted, liberally wet the butted ends. Fill the gaps between the sections with gobs of semistiff plaster. Add the plaster so it overlaps the gaps in such a way that the wall looks uniform.

With an X-acto knife, carve cracks and grooves from one casting to the other. Try to make the wall look uniform. By carefully plastering and carving, you can make the full length of the wall look like one continuous piece.

At this point you must decide if you like the sharp, straight-sided rocks left by the foil or if you prefer a rounded, weathered look. If you prefer the foil look, skip the next step.

The following procedures are followed to create the weathered look, fill in the air-bubble holes, add texture, and add a yellow-tan base color. Brush on a coat of water putty that has been mixed to a thin consistency, such as that of light cream. Don't make the mixture too thick, or a lot of cracks and grooves you want to keep will be filled and eliminated. The water putty sets fast, so mix

↗Fig. 9. LF&W's rock wall will be ¾" thick and will run 15 feet. Mount DuBarry, in background, was formed by the standard hardshell scenery technique. ↓Fig. 10. The installed castings are coated with water putty, then stained with thin washes of paint, blended for shading.

small quantities at a time — about a cupful. Because the consistency is thin and the setting time is fast, the putty has a tendency to dry with millions of tiny air bubbles. These mysteriously disappear, however, after the casting is stained.

Randomly stain the wall with thin washes of paint. Go easy here. It's not hard to put on too much color. If a goof is made, it can always be repaired by adding another coat of water putty. Several light coats of stain work best: burnt sienna, dark umber, tan, red, yellow, etc. I've had best results with oil-base or model paints such as diluted Floquil. Water-base paints don't work as well with the water putty. Apply several colors in random splotches. Let the color

run and blend together, so that there are gradual changes in shading. Work the darker stains into the cracks, crevices, and undersides of the rocks, to emphasize shadows. Leave the exposed edges and top light in color, to add to the illusion of depth. Add grass, shrubs, vines, or whatever, to give the wall personality.

A spinoff of this method is to make rocks by the hundreds. Leave out the paper reinforcing strips. When the plaster has hardened, break the casting into smaller subcastings. Add these to the scenery in the same way rock castings are used. It's even possible to cut the wall section with a coping saw so that specific shapes can be custom-fitted into specific places.

Felt grass and weeds

Another technique for our scenicking bag of tricks

BY ART CURREN

OVER the years new techniques and products have been offered by manufacturers and suggested by model railroad authors to make our scenery more realistic. Materials such as colored ground foam rubber, flock, twine, rope, or yarn fibers to represent grass, leaves, flowers, and the like have been introduced. All of them represent enormous improvements over dyed sawdust.

Let me offer one more addition to our bag of scenicking tricks: felt. I was looking for an easy method to make some ground cover that resembles thickly matted grass. Commercial products called "grass mat" are available (usually flock-covered rolls of paper), but I wanted something with taller grass that was not as neat and even as these grass mats. I also wanted something that would follow the contours of my basic scenery underlay better than the stiff paper backing of the grass mats.

It occurred to me that felt might be the answer. I purchased a few 9″ x 12″ swatches in the craft section of a hobby shop. After a little experimentation, I developed a few little techniques that give some variations to the height and texture of the grass, as well as some color variations, too.

I start out by using the color felt that's appropriate for the scene on which I'm working. For ordinary grass, I use olive-colored felt. Also, I have used the brighter greens, and I've even utilized tan to represent dead grass.

Next, I cut the felt to the right size and shape. I've found that cutting a zig-zag edge along the borders makes it easier to blend these into the area adjacent to the felt grass later on. Because of these zigs and zags, it's a good idea to texture the "under ground" at least ½″ inside the area the felt is to cover.

I apply spots of full-strength white glue to the back of the felt rather than on the ground surface. The glue need not cover the entire surface, but it should cover enough area to hold the felt securely in place. I'm careful not to get within ¼″ of the edges of the felt so the glue doesn't ooze out from underneath.

With the glue applied I place the felt down and press it into place, making it follow the contours of the ground form.

1   **2**   **3**

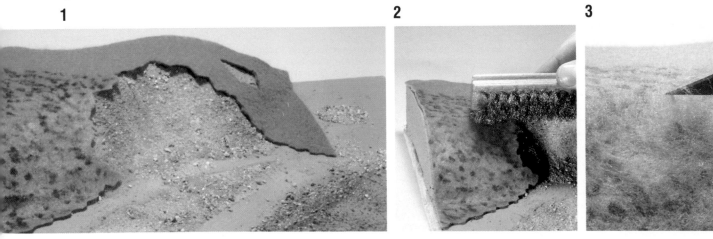

Leave it alone to dry properly for at least 30 to 45 minutes so it will be ready for the next steps.

Once the glue has dried and the felt is firmly bonded to the surface underneath it, I begin to add the color variation. As fig. 1 shows, I dab some darker green spots here and there with a wide-tip marking pen. Later on, you can apply pastel chalks or eye shadow colors if you feel you need still more color variation.

Next, I "tease" (you know, that's what your wife does to her hair to fluff it up) the felt with a brass-bristle suede shoe brush. I hold the brush so the bristles are parallel to the felt top and then pull upward, drawing up several of the compressed fibers. I keep doing this until I have created the look of tall grass. (I save the fuzzy tufts of fibers that get caught in the bristles for use later on). Figure 2 illustrates this technique.

Here and there I trade the brush for a hobby knife. By digging the tip into the felt and pulling it upward, I get quite a few individual fibers to come up even taller than those pulled up with the brush. See fig. 3. All of this teasing with both brush and hobby knife results in an uneven texture, exactly the look I am trying to achieve.

The edges need a little special treatment to blend them into the surrounding areas. Earlier I mentioned cutting zigzags into the edges; this is where that really helps. At the edges tease the felt outward rather than upward with both the brush and the knife. This "feathers" the edge into the dirt adjacent to the felt grass area. The zig-zags keep you from having a straight line where grass ends and dirt begins. The photo of the finished scene shows this effect.

Once I've finished the main grassy area, I add other weeds, bushes, and trees to provide additional texture, just as you would in any other scenery area. I cut a small X with a sharp blade where I want a tree or bush, and then I drill a hole in the center of the X. This prevents the fibers from twisting themselves around the drill. I put a dab of white glue in the hole to hold the tree or bush, and when the glue has dried, I tease the felt around the planted item to blend in the trunk or stem with the felt grass.

Earlier I mentioned that I saved the fuzzies that were caught in the bristles. Glue these down with a tiny dab of white glue a few scale inches beyond the edges of the felt area into the dirt. If you look again at the photo of the finished scene, I think you'll see that these little tufts help integrate the grassy area into the surrounding scenery.

Felt grass can also be added over existing scenery. The felt is flexible enough to be glued down over other surfaces, but make sure that you use enough white glue to bond the felt firmly. Where there may already be planted trees or bushes, cut the felt into patches to get around the trunks. A slit in the felt from one edge to the trunk works also. Tease the seams and they become practically invisible.

To be sure, felt grass is not as revolutionary as ground foam, but it is a very good supplementary technique to create a different texture in a scene. I don't suggest this as a technique you'd want to use over your whole layout. It would be both expensive and time-consuming. Instead, I recommend that you use it to enhance a special scene in areas where it can be seen "up close and appreciated."

Modeling LeWot Bog

A bath towel makes mighty fine swamp grass

BY ART CURREN

THAT'S "LeWot Bog," said the conductor to the rookie brakeman as their train rumbled past a small swamp. "What's so special about that?" the brakeman wondered.

The brakeman had a point: what is so special about a bog?

Well, bogs aren't particularly special, but they are very common, and that makes them likely candidates for miniaturization and inclusion on model railroads. Bogs may not have the splendor of rugged plaster mountains or majestic tree-laced hillsides, but they do have the appeal of being found almost anywhere in the United States, and often they are seen next to railroad tracks, since railroads frequently follow water to lessen grades. To gain truer realism in modeling, common scenic features, such as bogs, should be considered more often than they generally are. Those spectacular mountains can be easily over-modeled and appear toylike.

Such was my reasoning for miniaturizing LeWot Bog. Reasoning, however, is of no use without the means to perform it, so I thought I'd try a new method of construction utilizing something as common as a bog itself, a bath towel, to simulate the matted grasses and weeds. I'm lazy by nature, and the towel seemed an easy way to capture the feeling of a bog without implanting each tuft of grass or weeds one-by-one with a tweezers. That seemed like altogether too much effort to spend on a swamp, although I did "tweeze-in" a few rope and yarn fibers here and there.

Before actually getting around to trying the towel, I needed a bed for a lazy, barely flowing creek. I joined two 12"-square ceiling tiles, using a few scraps of 1"-square wood for cleats, and putting the good side of the tiles down so that the back, or rough side, would be my flat land.

A course for the water to follow was routed out, using a wire brush attachment in my 1" drill. The brush makes a nice, natural, rough texture in the soft tile. The depth of the stream ranges from $\frac{1}{8}$" to $\frac{1}{4}$" and the width varies between 1" and $1\frac{1}{2}$". I then brushed dark walnut stain over the creek bed and a few inches beyond to impart that dark, murky bottom that most bogs seem to have.

After the walnut stain had dried, I sealed the creek bed with a mist of diluted white glue mixed with a drop of detergent for spreading power. I used about one part glue to four or five parts water. Another mixture of thinned white glue (one part glue to one part water) was dribbled into the creek bottom, and then I sprinkled in a little sand, some small rocks, a few pebbles, and some assorted junk. I added a few shreds of green Scotch-Brite pot scrubber to simulate the undergrowth at the bottom. A few snips of jute twine were also sprinkled in at random.

Next, I made a small dam at each end of the bog so the "water" would not run off. Then I mixed and poured the stream, using Enviro-Tex, a two-part clear polymer resin. Although Enviro-Tex and similar products are primarily designed for producing shiny bar tops or finishing decoupage and craft projects, they are perfectly suited for simulating water.

The biggest advantage Enviro-Tex has over many other casting resins is that it has no offensive odor. Care should be taken to pour it in a well ventilated area, however.

While the water was setting up, which took three days, I turned to working with the bath towel. I began with a cocoa colored towel and used felt-tip markers to color it, using random strokes and alternating between two shades of light green. A nice, motley green began to emerge, just the thing for a mid-summer bog. The towel had too even a texture, so

I used scissors to shear a few portions in random fashion. This allowed some more of the cocoa color to show through, and I went over these areas with a few more strokes of the green markers if I felt the color had become too brown. Then I cut the toweling into pieces about 5 or 6 inches square with one edge cut to match the water's edge. I touched up the cut edges with a green marker.

To get an undulating ground surface, I glued small pieces of corrugated cardboard to the base here and there. Many times I used two layers to achieve vary-

ing heights. Where greater height was desired, scraps of wood elevated the contour even more. The towel has the capacity to stretch up and over these height variations, creating natural-looking contours. I used white glue straight from the bottle to secure the toweling to the ground surfaces.

Most of the joints between the towel sections could hardly be seen, but where there were gaps I added other foliage material, such as green-dyed filter material from a Kodak copy machine. Rope reeds filled some joints here and there and were used at the water's edge, as well as in the water itself after it had set enough to hold them upright.

In some preliminary experiments I had tried sections of carpet, but the fibers were too tall and too coarse to give the proper texture. Carpet may be usable in scales larger than HO, and my experiments were not entirely in vain, as I did use a few small scraps of carpet in LeWot Bog.

Felt-tip markers came into play again when I colored some of the other foliage materials. Brown and dark-green markers were stroked over 8- to 10-inch lengths of green yarn, jute twine, and common white string in random patterns to create a variety of tones in these "weeds." Short (½") lengths were then snipped off and the ends were fluffed up

with a dull knife before these weeds were planted into holes drilled into the soft tile. A variety of growth helps make the bog look jumbled and natural.

Since the toweling has a "grain" that scruffy look so common to bogs can be imparted by simply rubbing against the grain. Keeping all the grain going in the downstream direction can simulate the bog just after a spring flood or heavy rain, when fast-moving water has bent all the grasses in one direction. This is a difficult phenomenon to model, however, and the bog is more often seen in the calmer state, which I chose to capture.

As the ground begins to rise up out of the flat valley, foliage and trees can be modeled using more familiar materials such as ground foam and dyed sawdust. Many times the foliage bordering swamps

changes abruptly as the ground rises from the flat creek area and the soggy soil ends and drier soil begins. An abundance of heavy growth is found at this border due to the good footing for roots supplemented by the constant supply of water to support substantial growth.

LeWot (that's "towel" spelled backwards) Bog is a lot easier to make than a swamp made using the one-reed-at-a-time method. It may lack the super detail of the latter but I was able to complete my bog in less than three full evenings, exclusive of resin drying time. Today a bog; tomorrow, who knows? Wheat or grass fields might be made, using tan or yellow towels as a starting point, and I am sure other possibilities will come to mind as you enjoy the ease of the "LeWot" technique.

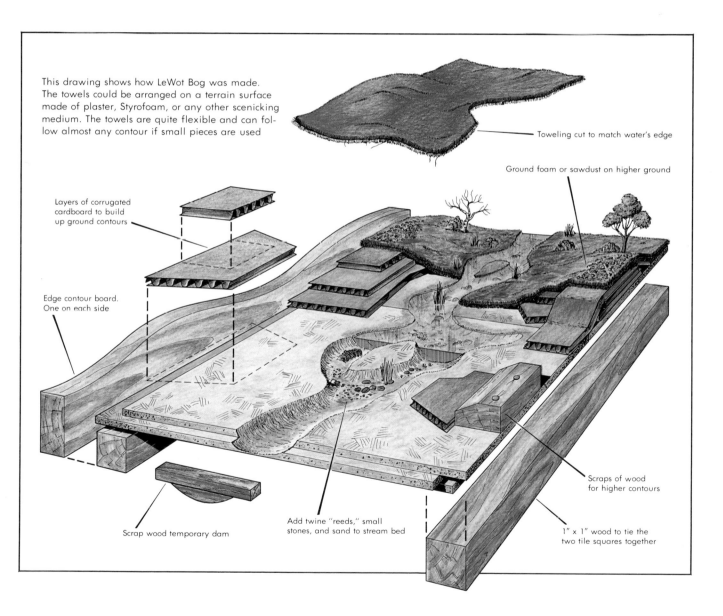

This drawing shows how LeWot Bog was made. The towels could be arranged on a terrain surface made of plaster, Styrofoam, or any other scenicking medium. The towels are quite flexible and can follow almost any contour if small pieces are used

Toweling cut to match water's edge

Ground foam or sawdust on higher ground

Layers of corrugated cardboard to build up ground contours

Edge contour board. One on each side

Scraps of wood for higher contours

Scrap wood temporary dam

Add twine "reeds," small stones, and sand to stream bed

1" x 1" wood to tie the two tile squares together

It's snowing again at Winter Park

BY BRIAN HOLTZ
PHOTOS BY A. L. SCHMIDT

WINTER PARK is a station I felt I had to include in my Panoramic Division model of the Denver & Rio Grande Western's Moffat Tunnel assault of the Rocky Mountains. With the west portal of the Moffat Tunnel, a passing track, and its role as a ski train destination, Winter Park is a prototype with both scenic and operating possibilities.

Those who have ridden the Rio Grande through the Moffat a few times know that the weather is often completely different at the two ends of the tunnel. I had decided to extend James Peak, the mountain over the tunnel, all the way to the ceiling of my railroad room, thus isolating Winter Park from the layout's east-slope scenes. By modeling a snow scene at the tunnel's west portal, I could use weather to emphasize the passage through the Continental Divide, at once calling attention to the purpose of the Panoramic Division and putting the "winter" in Winter Park.

PREPARING FOR WINTER

Although I hand laid the track on the rest of my main line, I used flextrack through Winter Park where the ties would be covered with snow. With the track in place, I built conventional hardshell scenery as described in Kalmbach's SCENERY FOR MODEL RAILROADS. I used profile boards of scrap fiberboard tacked to

The snow-covered west slope of the Rockies is the setting for a meet at Winter Park siding, left. Winter Park's snow contrasts with the scene at Cliff, above, on the mountains' eastern slope.

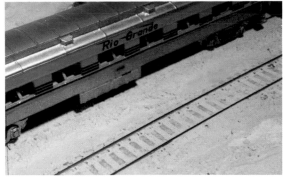

This touch-up job around the station demonstrates the snowfall technique used at Winter Park, a kind of zip-texturing with white plaster.

Modeling low snowbanks running along the tracks simulates the passage of plows or flangers. Be sure to clear the flangeways.

1 x 2 verticals to support some of the mountain peaks and taped in carefully arranged, crumpled newspapers to support the slopes and ski runs. Two layers of hardshell and a little extra over the thin spots provided a solid scenery base. I installed a few rock castings to represent outcroppings on nearly vertical surfaces.

The trees at Winter Park are mostly bumpy chenille as described in my October 1978 MR article. I found it much easier to glue the trees into small holes drilled in the hardshell and straighten them *after* the glue dried. The sequence goes like this: drill the holes, apply white glue in and slightly around each one, install the trees with a little more glue when the first application has pretty well set up, and straighten the trees when everything is dry. The wire in the bumpy chenille bends easily, although it took me an embarrassingly long time to figure that out.

I kept the trees to the steepest inclines to leave the flatter areas open as ski slopes. I also imposed a forced perspective on the scene by using bottle brush and a few Woodland Scenics trees up front, with progressively smaller bumpy chenille trees up the mountainside.

SNOWFALL

I started the cold weather effects with icicles cut from white paper for the Winter Park station. A thin coat of white glue gave the icicles a shiny surface, and when this dried, I white-glued the completed icicles to the eaves of the building. Once I had the station and a signal relay box installed, it was time for snow.

Modeling snow struck me as quite a challenge: the only permanently modeled snow scene I had ever come across was at Cold Shoulder on John Allen's Gorre & Daphetid RR. I began by testing a number of the plasters I had handy; the best representation of snow resulted from sprinkling on the whitest and finest-grained molding plaster. It's not as complicated as it might seem to those who have not tried it. I sprayed a fine mist of water over the entire scene, then sprinkled the plaster over everything through a fine strainer. Where more snow was needed, I applied more water mist and more molding plaster, a tablespoon at a time, until it looked right.

The only tools I used were a fine strainer, a tablespoon, a small paintbrush to move any misplaced snow, and a shop vacuum to clean up excess plaster that hadn't stuck.

The area beside the track was handled a little differently. I misted on water and applied dry plaster to cover the ties to a level slightly below the top of the rail. With a small ruler I smoothed the areas between the rails and directly beside the track to look as if a flanger or locomotive plow had shoved it to the side. This made small, continuous snowbanks alongside the track. Several passes of water mist held everything in place. I then cleaned out the flangeways with a knife and several pairs of old AHM wheelsets with oversized flanges and wiped up the excess plaster with paper towels.

In appropriate places I white-glued skiers, a snowman, and figures in winter clothes. Several N scale running figures and HO children in bright clothing were used to represent skiers at the higher elevations to assist the forced perspective.

SNOWSCAPES

Although it now looked pretty good to the eye, my first attempts at photographing the Winter Park scene were disappointing. There was absolutely no depth, because the scene lacked the play of light and shadow we see in real snowscapes. In frustration I diluted black dye with water and sprayed it onto the areas where I wanted shadows. I figured that if it failed, I could add more white plaster over the top when it had dried.

To my surprise, the diluted black dye didn't change the appearance immediately. The molding plaster can accept quite a bit of it. I made repeated applications, and slowly the depth I was hoping for appeared. It still looked like snow — and not dirty snow — but now it had realistic shadows. The photos turned out with the depth I had hoped for.

SNOW GROOMING

The scene has been on my layout for more than 2½ years and requires no more maintenance than the rest of my scenery. I clean up dust with a shop vacuum, with an old nylon stocking over the opening (for a second chance at anything that I might not want to lose, like people or trees that have come loose). For spot touch-up I just use the mist and strained white molding plaster. If it becomes too thick, I simply chip away some of the old plaster with a modeling knife and make it snow again. ₲

Gregg Condon built the station from photos, and the author added brick texture and weather effects.

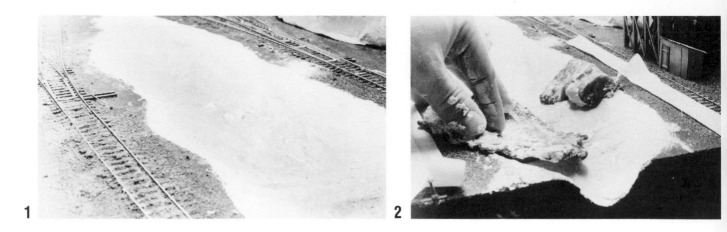

1

2

Modeling Furlow's Slough

A beginner can get his feet "wet" with this project

BY MALCOLM FURLOW

THE Wind River Branch of Jim Findley's Tioga Pass RR., is on a windswept plateau surrounded by rugged beauty. Nestled against a backdrop of majestic mountains, the little branch line provides most of the ore traffic handled by the Tioga Pass. Jim reports that cinnabar is mined in great quantities along the line, and a little logging is also done from time to time.

Runoff coming down from the high terrain has been caught in a natural depression called "Furlow's Slough." This water has caused many a problem, with spring rains continually overrunning the banks of the slough, flooding both track and roadbed. This costs the little railroad money that it should be spending on upgrading some of its derelict equipment.

Sadly, the slough has also become a dumping ground for discarded barrels and rusty old mining machinery. (Mine operators in the area haven't learned about ecology and environmental health yet!)

FORMING THE BASE

Furlow's Slough is a good project for a newcomer to get his feet wet in the use of casting resin. The area to be modeled is not large, so the amount of resin required is small. (Resin sometimes becomes a messy chore on larger projects.)

Begin construction by forming the base for the slough. Cut a hole in the tabletop to allow a 1″ depression. Jim used plaster-impregnated gauze (like doctors use to make a cast) to form the slough base shown in fig. 1. This technique is unfamiliar to me, so on my own layout I use the traditional Hydrocal/paper towel method. Regardless of the method you use to form the base, be *sure* that there are no holes for the casting resin to find its way through. This stuff will find the *smallest* hole and begin leaking. It's also smart to place an ample amount of newspaper under the layout just in case.

Before beginning work on the scenery, apply masking tape over any nearby track, especially if you are working on a friend's layout! While I was applying ground cover around the slough, a little diluted white glue found its way into one of Jim's three-way turnouts and effectively made it inoperative. I still bear the marks caused by the incident. Anyway, use some tape and hopefully it won't happen to you. (Try add-

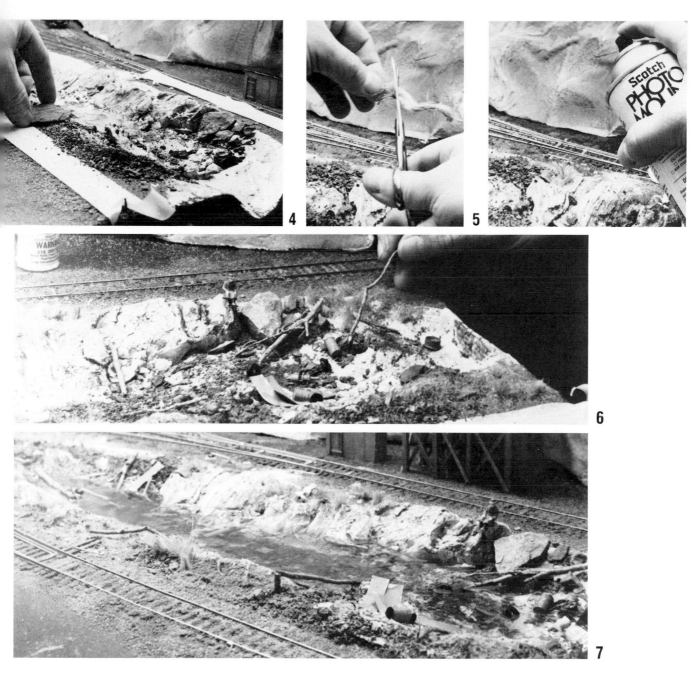

ing a drop or two of oil on the moving parts of any turnout located close to an area to be scenicked. It will help keep the parts from being plastered together.)

DETAILING THE SLOUGH BASE

Figure 2 shows how we used molds along the banks to create a rugged edge. The castings are stained using India ink and water, and colored with acrylics. Jim later went back and darkened the rock castings a bit to match his scenery color. The castings can also be dry-brushed to bring out highlights.

We colored the bottom of the depression to match the decomposed granite we added, along with larger stones placed here and there for effect. See fig. 3. Avoid letting the larger stones overpower the small body of water.

We detailed the banks using the same decomposed granite used in the slough bottom, plus Woodland Scenics ground foam and Boyd Models electrostatic grass. Be

sure to use white glue diluted with water (1:1 ratio) to secure the ground cover in the slough bed. This will keep funny little bubbles from forming when you pour the casting resin.

Weeds play an important part in detailing an area such as this, and we used a lot of macrame fibers to represent this vegetation. See fig. 4. Scotch photo-mount spray glue (fig. 5) held most of the weeds in place; a later application of some diluted white glue made everything permanent.

A few rusty old barrels and corrugated roofing panels placed here and there gave the slough a little character. Broken twigs were used to represent logs. The detailed slough bottom is shown in fig. 6.

POURING THE RESIN

After everything is securely in place and the glue has set, it's time to pour the casting resin. The casting resin I used was made by Natcol Crafts Inc. Be sure to tape any areas where the slough base might

reach the table edge, forming a sort of dam to keep the resin back. Be sure to provide adequate ventilation before pouring.

Mix the resin according to the manufacturer's directions, adding a bit of extra hardener. This will create a wavy effect due to the added heat. Pour the resin to a depth of ⅛" to ¼", allowing each layer to set before pouring in another batch. You might want to add a little blue-green dye to the resin for some color. Just a drop or two of dye is all that is needed.

Our slough took three coats of resin; we added dye to the last two batches. The actual amount of resin required will depend on the depth of the depression you will be covering. If you think a greater feeling of depth is required, use more green dye, rather than more resin. The completed slough is shown at fig. 7.

Jim and I had a great time constructing Furlow's Slough, especially the time we spent trying to unstick the points on his three-way turnout! ⚙

You can model realistic-looking prairie grass like this using the author's soft-shell scenery methods for fake fur that are described in this article. In this scene on Bronsky's HO scale Skokie River Valley module, two North Shore express motors are hauling freight to Skokie Valley customers.

Modeling tall prairie grass

Using fake fur for soft-shell scenery makes flat terrain come alive

BY ERIC BRONSKY
PHOTOS BY THE AUTHOR

WHEN we think of model railroad scenery, a mental image of rugged terrain usually forms. Lofty mountains and spectacular gorges, not flat boards, are what make layouts appear interesting and seem larger. We learned this space-expanding philosophy from expert modelers since before John Allen's time, and even today scenic artists like Malcolm Furlow are inspiring folks to build tunnels and trestles galore.

Those of us who faithfully model certain railroads of Illinois, Kansas, and other plains states, however, are faced with the challenge of creating interesting scenery on a fairly level surface. In parts of the Midwest the pancake-flat topography is broken only by river valleys, an occasional knoll, or man-made structures. Vast prairies and farm fields, dotted with just a few trees and shrubs, often stretch on for miles.

Such was the case with the now-abandoned Chicago North Shore & Milwaukee RR's Skokie Valley Route, whose arrow-straight right-of-way shot through 18 miles of northern Illinois flatlands. Being an ardent North Shore fan, and having already modeled a few structures which stood along this stretch, I decided to incorporate my HO scale structures into a fully scenicked portable module.

Overall, the module measures 18" x 48" and is designed to interface with operating modules built by fellow modelers in my club, the Northwest Traction Group. Because I hope to eventually build a large, permanent North Shore system, I decided to use this small area as a testing ground for the scenery techniques which are the subject of this article.

There must be a dozen different ways to model the wild grasses which thrive here and there, principally in the plains states.

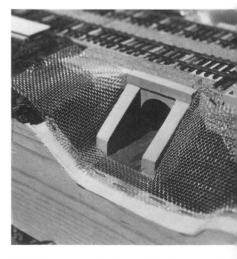

Fig. 1. The foundation for soft-shell scenery is galvanized screen wire. After the screeen is cut and stapled in place, the fake fur is glued to it.

Modelers have been using yarn, twine, ground foam, roughed-up felt, terry cloth, lichen, and even human hair with varying results. Hardly a year goes by that some skilled scenery virtuoso doesn't come up with a new and interesting technique. But one trait which most of these techniques have in common is that the foliage has to be placed on the layout in small, individual clumps. This is a time-consuming and tedious chore, especially if a large area has to be covered.

My approach is just the opposite. I glue down entire "fields" of fake fur and cut away unwanted material. I then color and blend the fur with other scenic materials. This sequence seems odd because most folks are used to creating a basic ground texture first and then adding grass and other foliage afterwards, as is done in the hardshell method. Because my technique doesn't even require a rigid plaster crust, I suppose it would be appropriate to adopt the term "soft-shell" scenery. For creating tall grass or marshy areas ranging in size from a few square inches to several square yards, the realism of soft-shell scenery makes flat terrain come alive.

MATERIAL

You can buy fake fur at fabric stores for about $8.50 a yard. I purchased one yard, and it was more than I needed for my module. Fake fur comes in a variety of colors, but the only shade available at the time of my purchase was a golden honey-wheat. Strangely enough, this is an excellent color to work with. It closely resembles yellow or burnt grass and might have been left in its natural state had I desired this effect on my module.

Chances are you won't find the exact same fabric, but the sort of material you'll need is a polyester pile whose fibers are at least ½" long. It should be coarse enough that the fibers can be fluffed up and will remain standing. Avoid any material with a downy or limp texture, and choose a pastel shade of off-white, gold, beige, or light green instead of a dark or intense shade which would be impossible to color realistically.

The longer and hairier furs have a tendency to shed like a gorilla in a heat wave, so store the fabric in a box or plastic bag until you're ready to use it. Don't be put off by the fact that it more resembles an animal hide than a prairie at this stage.

If you're unable to locate a source of suitable fake fur, Scentare Inc., P. O. Box 27928, Tempe, AZ 85282, makes a prairie grass mat for model railroad use. Many of the techniques described in this article can be used to heighten the realism of this product, too.

SCENERY SUPPORTS

I constructed my basic modular framework out of 1 x 4s and used ½" plywood for the subroadbed. Contours for the riverbed were sawn into the front and rear members. Other than a few scraps of plywood added beneath structures and the roadway, the rest of the framework was left open.

I recommend using wire screen to support the grassy areas. Screen is flexible enough to bend into nearly any contour and yet is sturdy enough to hold its shape. You can form gentle slopes and rolling contours without having to build up or cut away flat surfaces. A sheet plywood or Homasote tabletop, on the other hand, costs more and adds a considerable amount of unnecessary weight.

Figure 1 shows how I fitted screen wire around the Skokie River culvert in the narrow space between subroadbed and the front edge of my module. In areas where much larger sections of screening are needed, scraps of wood nailed to the framing members will provide adequate support as well as sturdy anchor points for the scenery. Transitional pieces and contours can be built up using scraps of Styrofoam, cork, or balsa. The latter materials will also come in handy wherever rigid support is needed for tree trunks or utility poles, as I shall describe later.

Riverbeds, rocky outcroppings, and anything else that might entail some messy plasterwork should be completed before you even think about putting down any turf. I used the conventional plaster-over-

Fig. 3. Cut the fur with the cloth side face up as shown. Use only the tips of the scissors to nibble at the material so the fibers along the edge of the cut don't get trimmed away inadvertently.

Fig. 4. Combing out the loose fur is just like grooming a pet, except that the fake fur doesn't bite. This step improves the looks of the grass.

screen-wire method to create a bed for the Skokie River. It was necessary to extend the plaster up the side of the banks a bit to contain the clear casting resin which I poured later.

PLANTING THE GRASS

Cutting the fabric to size and cementing it in place is a rather hairy task (GROAN!). The simplest approach is to transfer the dimensions of odd-size areas from your layout to the material using paper templates. Figure 2 shows one such template being readied. Making all the templates at one time and laying these out together on the fabric will eliminate much trial-and-error trimming and thus reduce waste.

Whatever you do, keep in mind that each template has an "up" and a "down" side. Mark these so they don't get reversed unintentionally. Place the "up" sides face-down against the fabric backing and use a felt-tip pen to trace around the edges.

The next step is to take a sharp scissors with blades tapering to a point and cut out the pieces of fur in such a way that the fibers along the cut edge don't get cropped short. See fig. 3. At this stage the stuff will begin to shed like crazy, so as soon as the pieces are cut, put away all scraps and leftover material. Run a comb vigorously through the fur several times to remove all the loose fuzz. See fig. 4. Test fit the pieces on your layout to make sure the edges will end up exactly where you want them.

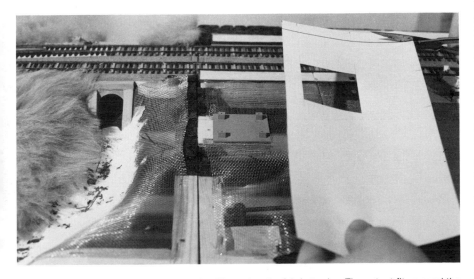

Fig. 2. A paper template can be used to simplify cutting the fabric to size. The cutout fits around the base of a high-tension tower. The plaster riverbed was installed before the fake fur was added.

Fig. 5. At this stage the fur doesn't resemble prairie grass any more than a Mikado resembles a Geep. But it will look like grass after it has been cut, colored, and blended with other scenic materials.

MOWING THE LAWN

Unless you are deliberately modeling a well-manicured lawn, the one thing you should avoid when trimming extra-long fur to a more realistic height is uniformity. Wild grasses tend to grow in clumps or patches and may vary in height from a few inches up to 8 feet. When you view an open field from a distance, all the grass seems fairly uniform in height and density. But in confined areas like those between tracks or buildings, the variation is much more apparent. Some prototype examples are shown in fig. 6.

There are fake furs available whose fibers are the right scale length for our purposes. But to achieve a truly realistic effect, I recommend that you start with the longest, hairiest stuff you can find, and then cut it down to different lengths. If you're modeling a fairly large field, an electric clipper will make a dandy lawnmower, but again the result might appear too uniform on a small area or in the foreground.

Would you believe I trimmed all the fur on my Skokie Valley module with a scissors and comb? I used the comb to rake the fibers upright after every few snips to check my progress. I wanted the grass to average out to a scale 3-foot height, so this meant clipping off approximately ½" of material. The whole job took me a couple hours but was really a lot less tedious than the "clump-at-a-time" method.

Whichever utensils you choose, experiment on a scrap piece first. Work with a small section at a time and check your progress at eye level every few minutes. Once you've finished hacking your way through a section, comb it and use a vacuum cleaner to pick up the loose clippings. Then go over your work as a barber would with a customer — blend, add highlights, and clip off any stray strands.

Be careful not to cut the fibers so short that the cloth backing becomes clearly visible through the fur. But don't worry if you end up with a few bald spots here and there. You can disguise these spots later by adding bits of foliage material or ground cover. In fact, this is

The adhesive I used to plant my turf is not really an adhesive at all but a water-soluble artist's medium called acrylic molding paste. This white, nearly odorless paste can be found at most art supply stores. It has the consistency of texture paint when wet and forms a tough but pliable bond when dry. Unlike contact cement, its main advantage is the generous amount of working time you'll have to position and adjust the fabric before the paste sets. And unlike runny glues, the paste will stay put on the backing and not permeate the fibers.

Using a paintbrush, apply unthinned molding paste directly to the fabric backing. On pieces more than 4" wide there is no need to coat the entire surface; a 2"-wide band of paste around the perimeter will do. Application should be generous, but not to the point where excess globs ooze out when you press the material in

place. Also, don't try to work with more than one piece at a time.

Getting the fur to conform to the contours of the wire screen is no problem. The cloth backing has elastic properties and can be stretched. You might have to place weights over some areas along the edge to keep them down until the paste hardens. To pull the fur down into concave areas where there is no adhesive, make up twist ties out of bits of fine wire. Bend the wire into a tight U shape and insert it through the fur and screen wire, tying it off beneath the screen.

The molding paste hardens in a matter of hours, and you'll be amazed at its strong adhesive properties. At this stage your efforts will resemble a bathroom rug more than a stretch of prairie. See fig. 5. But take heart; the next two steps will almost magically transform this unearthly fuzz into blades and waves of tall grass.

Fig. 6. Above. Here's an example of yellow or "dead" grass along the Kansas City Southern's right-of-way. **Left.** The Chicago Surface Lines' Stony Island route ran through fields of typically tall, uniformly dense prairie grass, interrupted only by occasional clusters of weeds. This photograph was taken in late spring or early summer.

R. W. Gibson

Fig. 7. Above, left. This is what the fake fur grass looks like right after it has been glued down — not very realistic-looking yet. **Above, right.** This is the same area of the author's module after the "grass" has been colored, trimmed, and fluffed up. Other scenery materials will be added next.

a good way to simulate a somewhat sparser growth. Another approach would be to do some of the trimming with a barber's thinning shears.

COLORING

Just as prairie grasses vary in height, there are also subtle variations in color. This is most apparent when you look down at a field from a higher elevation. Well maintained lawns usually have a continuous rich green tone, but wild grasses are predominantly pale green with yellowish or brownish splotches and occasional bursts of brighter colors. For modeling purposes, the best approach is to start by tinting the fur green and then working in some secondary colors.

The fur should be colored in such a way that the fibers don't clump or mat together permanently. Several different alternatives are possible using diluted paint, ink, or fabric dye. I chose to use

what I'm most familiar with, namely Floquil paints. But there shouldn't be any problem with other coloring agents as long as they can be thinned out to a wash consistency. Once again, I suggest that you experiment first.

I sampled a number of different shades before settling on Floquil's R-36 Weyerhauser Green. This green is not a very realistic foliage color by itself, but when diluted to wash consistency and combined with my straw-colored fur, the resulting blend of color looks and photographs convincingly.

Two different techniques for coloring the fur are possible. My approach was to glob a brushload or two of paint straight from the jar onto a 6"-square area. I then dipped a large, stiff sash brush into a container of Dio-Sol and applied a scrubbing motion to the area, diluting the color and saturating the fibers at the same time. The intensity and evenness

of the color was regulated by the amount of paint and solvent I applied, thus providing a wide range of subtle variations in tone and hue.

The other method is to premix the paint and solvent to the consistency of a tint or wash. Saturate the fur thoroughly with a large brush. The fibers *will* mat, although not permanently, at this stage. Be sure to wear old clothes and cover everything in the immediate vicinity with drop cloths or newspaper because this stuff spatters in all directions. Also, work in a well ventilated area if using Floquil paints. If that's not possible, try using water-base paints or fabric dyes.

Keep in mind that in nature, riverbanks and places where water would be likely to collect after a storm are a more intense green, while hilltops and areas receiving less moisture and no protection from the sun appear parched. So

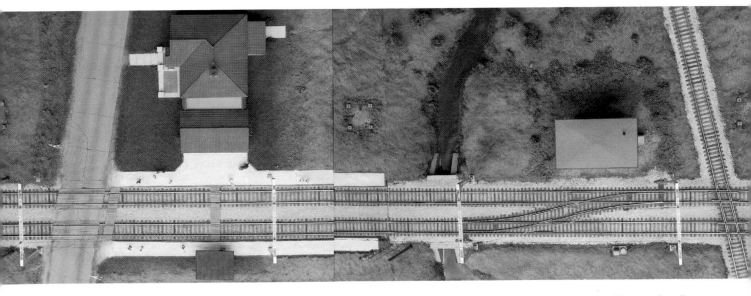

Fig. 8. Here's a bird's-eye view of the entire module after all scenery work had been completed. The effectiveness of careful blending is apparent. The right portion can be compared to photos in fig. 7. The overall realism was further enhanced by weathering the structures, road, and ballast.

ETCHED BRASS FOLIAGE

ABOUT HALFWAY through this project I learned of Scale Link, a company in England which manufactures structural kits and detail parts. They specialize in brass photoetchings, and their line includes a surprisingly wide assortment of highly detailed photoetched *plants* in both 4-mm and 7-mm scales, which correspond roughly to HO and O scales. Seven different types of foliage for trees and shrubs are available, along with a selection of small, nonwoody plants.

Scale Link products are available in the U. S. from VLS Warwinds International, West Port Industrial Parks, 804 Fee Fee Road, Maryland Heights, MO 63043. The photoetched sheets are roughly $6 each; A catalog is available.

For my module I obtained sheets F-42, "Oak leaf" foliage, and F-41, "Pond and canal plants." The manufacturer recommends painting the entire sheet before cutting out individual pieces. I didn't have any suitable green paint on hand and ended up mixing my own, but you'll find that military camouflage greens generally blend well with the other scenic materials.

After spraying both sides of the etched sheets, I hand-painted the tree branches and rushes brown.

Scale Link photoetched plants were strategically placed along the water's edge to finish this foreground scene.

The next step was to separate the individual plants and bend them into a realistic three-dimensional form. Care must be taken because some of the narrower stems and branches are very fragile. The pond and canal plants can be completed and ready to install in a matter of minutes. The tree foliage, on the other hand, consists of hundreds of leaves, and *each one* must be twisted this way or that. I found this to be so tedious that I prepared only enough sprigs to complete a partial tree, which served as a photographic prop.

Such exquisitely detailed foliage is best appreciated when well lit and placed in the foreground.

after you're done with the basic green tint, go back and highlight these special areas. Some useful secondary colors include Floquil Earth, Concrete, and Reefer White (or their equivalents if you're working with a different medium). If you're unhappy with the results at any stage, merely saturate the area with more solvent to thin out the previously applied color and then splash on some new color.

Let the fur dry for a day or two, and then fluff it up with a comb. The nondescript pile of matted green fuzz will instantly turn into a lush prairie, right before your eyes! The "before" and "after" views in fig. 7 show the breadth of this transformation. Later, you may get the urge to make some areas greener or perhaps add a brownish spot. You can apply more color at any time.

SCENIC BLENDING

One of the keys to making soft-shell scenery appear realistic is the manner in which the artificial fur is blended with adjacent scenic elements. Wherever wild grass meets a man-made barrier such as a sidewalk, fence, or structure, it comes to an abrupt edge. But transitions elsewhere are more gradual. On my module I had to devise subtle ways of blending the fur into the roadbed, riverbanks, patches of bare earth, and areas scenicked with ground foam.

I discovered early in my project that Woodland Scenics' ground foam, available in several different textures and shades of green, makes an excellent blending

Fig. 9. The author achieved a realistic transition between the station lawn and the prairie grass by using loose ground foam. This material looks more natural if applied unevenly. Somewhat less prototypical is Bronsky's model of a Boeing LRV in the background painted for the North Shore.

Left. This is what Scale Link's etched brass foliage sheets look like after they're painted. Under close examination you can see that Scale Link has etched individual stems and veins into each leaf. **Above.** Here is what the individual etched plants look like after being carefully separated from the sheets. In the top row there are reeds, bullrushes, and foxglove. The bottom row contains ferns, arrowheads, and wild cabbages.

medium. In fact, the "burnt grass" turf material turned out to be an almost exact match to the color of my fur after tinting. Several other products in their line, have also proved useful.

To blend tall prairie grass into other landscaped areas, be they well maintained lawns or dense forests, the trimming procedure differs somewhat from the one already described. You can cement the fur directly over existing scenery. However, if you're starting with an unscenicked section, staple or tack the edge of the screen wire so that it overlaps approximately ½" into the adjoining areas. Cut the edges of the fur in an irregular pattern. The material need not line up with the edge of the screen.

While you're playing barber, contour the borders of the fur by cutting in a smooth taper rather than leaving an abrupt drop-off to the adjoining scenery. Then proceed to tint the fur. Once all traces of solvent or moisture evaporate, get the following items together:

● At least two shades of ground-foam turf material, in both fine and moderately coarse textures. Choose colors that will blend realistically with the color of the adjacent scenery.

● Supplies and utensils for bonding scenic materials using diluted polymer matte medium. [This water-soluble scenery method is described by Dave Frary is his book *How to Build Realistic Model Railroad Scenery* (Kalmbach).]

Start by sprinkling the coarse foam along the edge of the fur, and then cover a wider area with a layer of fine turf. Any unwanted ruts or depressions can be filled in with more loose foam. Avoid the temptation to be neat; carry the foam well over into the furry area and try not to apply it uniformly. If the results don't look realistic, simply vacuum up or sprinkle on more foam until you're satisfied.

When all looks good, fill a sprayer bottle with water and add a drop or two of detergent. Spray the foam until it's saturated. Next, apply a dilution of 1 part polymer matte medium to 5 parts water to the loose material, using a medicine dropper. Although the dropper method is tedious, it gives you better control than a spray bottle in applying the bonding agent where it's needed. Water alone won't matt the fibers, but use the matte medium sparingly around the fur. The scenery will look positively dreadful during this stage, but don't disturb it because when the milky liquid dries it's invisible.

Figure 9 shows a typical fur-to-foam transition on my module. The site immediately surrounding my Sheridan Elms station had been landscaped a few years earlier. After completing the basic blending, I added some larger bits of foam and loose tufts of fiber.

The areas beneath my high-tension towers and South Upton Tower were scenicked with real sand and gravel. Here, too, I used ground foam to effect a natural transition to tall grass. All gaps between the ballasted roadbed and fur were likewise filled in with loose foam.

The Skokie River posed a problem because I intended to use clear casting resin for the water, but didn't want to embed the edges of the fur in this stuff. I let the fur remain untrimmed and unattached along the river's edge, as shown in fig. 7, so that I could pin it back when I was ready to pour the resin. Only after the plastic had hardened did I trim the material along the banks and glue the fabric down with acrylic molding paste. Finally, ground foam was used effectively here as elsewhere to fill in spots between the grass and water.

ADDING FOLIAGE

A typical prairie contains many other forms of plant life besides grasses. If the botanists in the audience will pardon my greenhouse English, I shall categorize all of this miscellaneous flora as flowers, shrubs, and weeds.

Modeling shrubbery and weeds is simplified by the many versatile foliage materials available. At a few places on my module I glued down Woodland Scenics' foam-covered mesh, stretched thin so that the tall grass poked its way through in spots. This created the effect of dense patches of underbrush choking the growth of tall grass. Elsewhere, I added small individual shrubs made from the same material, placed singly or in clumps. For more variety, lichen and other materials can also be worked in effectively.

Installing trees and shrubs over unsupported screen wire is a bit tricky because something has to be placed underneath to hold the trunks upright. The easiest solution is to cut a sheet of Styrofoam into small blocks, put globs of molding paste on top, and hold these against the underside of the screen while you push the trunks into place. Use an awl to poke holes for the trunks, because drills will only snag and get tangled up in the fibers. Some temporary supports might be needed until the paste hardens.

Flowering weeds can be simulated by a number of methods, depending on the effect you want. Here and there I sprinkled patches of fine ground foam onto my module and affixed them with tiny droplets of diluted matte medium. In a few places I whisked a brush dipped in white, yellow, or lavender paint through the very tops of the fibers. And wherever I desired an accent in the form of a splash of bolder color, such as along the river, I glued down a shred of autumn-colored foliage to represent a clump of wild flowers.

Figure 8 is a bird's-eye view of my entire module as it appeared at this stage. Note the placement of scenic elements as well as the subtle blending of texture and color. Its realism is due in part to my conscious effort to avoid intense colors and uniformity. Prairie modeling doesn't have quite the scenic impact of a Rocky Mountains pass, but it need not be dull either.

When folks view my module, they almost invariably run their fingers through the grass. After a few hundred moist, clammy pawings, I'm afraid my scenery is going to resemble the aftermath of a locust attack. Perhaps the best solution would be to add yet another superdetail in the form of authentic ragweed pollen. This might not make a visible difference to the prairie grass, but it should induce one heck of a prototype sneeze! ✿

Turn asparagus fern into corn

There's no magic in this "corny" little trick

BY J. F. VAN WICKEL JR.

WALLACE'S FARM is one of the newer developments on the HO Hemmit Valley Lines, occupying a corner once intended as a quarry but subsequently filled in. Once I had subjected it to a liberal treatment of selective compression, Revell's original farm complex (left over from my son Rick's layout) just fit the space. The garden area, however, needed some tall corn, which is not readily available in HO. Having grown several rows of sweet corn in our 12-inch-to-the-foot garden, I at least knew what it looked like and felt qualified to model the maize.

While poking around in a craft supply shop one day, I stumbled onto some plastic asparagus fern which had the appropriate branching, if not the correct shape. See fig. 1. A little experimentation led to an acceptable HO corn plant. The accompanying photos illustrate the technique, but unless you're a brute for punishment, I'd suggest limiting this effort to a typical small-farm garden plot. A normal Iowa-type cornfield would take up time better spent finishing up a Shay or building a pickle-car kit.

From the stock select end pieces with a nice vertical spike. Cut them to about 7 scale feet and trim them roughly to the shape shown in fig. 2. Next grab each plastic "leaf" (not the central spike) with a flat-nosed pliers and mash it flat. (Don't be fooled. Real craftsmanship isn't required here; nor is a particularly delicate touch.)

Figure 3 shows the start of the only truly critical operation in the making of model maize. With a needle-nose or round-nose pliers, taper the thickness of each leaf from the stalk out to the leaf tips. Next, with a small pair of fine-pointed cuticle scissors, trim each leaf to a lance-like shape. Keep tapering each leaf, both in thickness and in width, until your plant looks like the one in fig. 4.

Incidentally, those fierce teeth in the picture belong to the alligator clamp on a rather clever gadget called the "Portable Hand," which is great for holding small objects. (In this case, I used the device to hold the corn stalks *and* the tools for the close-up time exposures.)

Make about two or three dozen stalks and you're ready for planting. Wallace's garden soil is texture paint over Masonite and is contoured in three rows about 2 or 3 scale feet apart. I prefer the slower-setting texture paint for scenery because it gives you more time to shape and reshape. After the cornfield dries, drill appropriate-size holes every ¼" or so apart and set the stalks.

A real purist would retouch the plastic to get the yellowing leaf tips typical of mature corn. Further, he would neatly insert $1/87$ scale ears of corn in their husks (approximately 0.14") at the leaf-to-stalk junctures. Simulating the silk protruding from the husks (about .001") would require fibers smaller than any I have found, and so I leave this up to the next modeler's ingenuity. I avoided these fine touches, since my basic railroading policy is to leave a little something unfinished to keep the critics happy.

I haven't tried creating a cornfield in N scale, and I'll bet in Z scale it would be a real wall-climbing challenge. Or should I say a corn-siderable effort? ✿

1

2

3

4

Creating a fall scene

BY DEAN FOSTER

THE SHADOWS are long and dark, and the frost is on the pumpkin. Well, actually there aren't any pumpkins in the field on my fall scene, but there *are* the dried up cornstalks so typical of the fall of the year.

What you see in the photo is about all there is (a 2 x 4-foot diorama), but the same materials and techniques I used to build the diorama could be used to build an entire layout that features fall scenery.

The bases for the diorama and background hills were carved out of Styrofoam blocks with a hot wire. This must be done *outdoors*, or if necessary, indoors but with extremely good ventilation (i.e., open windows and a strong fan), as the gas produced is poisonous. Hills and valleys are quickly shaped this way, taking much less time than is needed to build plaster scenery.

Following the hot wire treatment, I paint the Styrofoam with an earth-colored latex, using a brush. While the paint is still wet, I sprinkle on ground foam and dyed sawdust for grass and weeds. When the latex dries the greenery is "glued" in place on the layout.

Should you eventually decide that the scene needs more ground cover, all you need to do is sprinkle on some more and then spray it with a mixture of 3:1 water/white glue from a household spray bottle. When you've finished for the day, remove the spray top from the bottle and run fresh water through it so that no glue sets up in the nozzle parts.

I made the trees from the flower part of a wild bush common here in southern California. Very likely similar natural "trees" can be found in all parts of the country. These are simply pressed into the Styrofoam hillsides; then the tops are sprayed with orange paint from an aerosol can. Spray small sections at a time (again, outdoors or with proper ventilation) and sprinkle on the foliage while the paint is wet. Use various shades of red, orange, and yellow foliage so that there is a variety of color rather than uniformity.

I made the leaves from finely sifted sawdust dyed with Tintex cloth dyes: Red Red no. 50 and Brilliant Yellow no. 5. By combining these two basic colors in different proportions, you obtain a range of reds, oranges, and yellows. Dissolve 1 tablespoon of dye in 1 pint of warm water, and add sawdust until all of the liquid is absorbed. Spread this on a thick sheet of newspaper and lay it in the sun to dry.

The corn plants are actually the dry seed stalks of a wild grass. In nature the stalks are from 4" to 6" long, so I cut them up with a scissors into scale 6- to 7-foot pieces (the average height of corn plants). I poke holes in the Styrofoam in neat rows 3 scale feet apart, and then with a tweezers, I plant the stalks in each row 1 foot apart from one another.

You're absolutely right; the cornfield does take a while to complete. But I think it's worth doing for a couple of reasons: first, it's a detail you don't often see on layouts; and second, along with the orange, red, and yellow trees, the dried up cornfield helps to set the season of your layout. ◘

Bushes for your layout

A simple method for making realistic shrubbery

BY JOHN NEHRICH

PHOTOS BY THE AUTHOR

DESPITE advances in model railroad scenery material and techniques, we still have a long way to go in modeling specific plant life — grasses, shrubbery, trees. At present, the best I can do is suggest foliage, using as many materials and methods as possible to create the impression of diversity.

Leaves are the source of greenery for all trees and other foliated plant life. While identical in basic function, both leaves and supporting structure vary in appearance tremendously from species to species.

The Rensselaer Model Railroad Society has used a variety of synthetic fibers for leaf material on the club's New England, Berkshire & Western layout — things such as fake fur, synthetic fibers, and commercial ground foams. The latter product bears the brunt of suggesting foliage.

While foam-covered lichen makes adequate bushes, there is a much easier way of making an airy and open-looking plant arrangement. We got the idea from Bill Kennedy, who used this technique on his Rampo Valley layout some years ago. It is amazing how fast and simple the technique is, and how realistic the result.

The basic material is poly fiber, a plastic thread material that looks like steel wool. We have used a tree kit product called See-Niks Fibre (made by AHM but no longer available). Bachmann has a similar product called Poly Fibre.

Because of the see-through nature of these bushes, the ground surface is visible, so you'll need to prepare it with a covering of Boyd Electrostatic Grass or any of the commercial grass materials.

Take the poly fiber and stretch it out over the scenery into a cloud-like formation. Spray it heavily with hair spray and sprinkle on fine ground foam. Woodland Scenics' Blended Turf is good, but use other colors for variation. Give a couple of extra sprays after the foam is in place to secure it to the poly fiber. Simple, isn't it?

It takes a little while to realize just how tenuously the bushes are held in place. Catch a few strands of the foliage net and you can defoliate a whole area. If you try to drill a hole for a utility pole in the midst of a clump of bushes, all you get is an empty plot and a drill bit looking like a fork wrapped with spaghetti. If the bushes are too close to the tracks, a local freight may snag itself a bridal train. To prevent this form of defoliation, I plant some grass between bushes and track. This acts as a barrier between the trains and the bushes, and in the bargain, provides some of that desired scenic contrast. ✿

Stretch the poly fiber over the ground cover by pulling on it. Vary the height and density as shown. Apply hair spray and a coat of ground foam. The result is a most realistic-looking clump of bushes.

John Nehrich

A source for large pine trees

Check out those post-Christmas sales

BY JOHN NEHRICH

THE PINE trees along the right-of-way of the New England, Berkshire & Western (Rensselaer Model Railroad Society layout) are of the bottle-brush type. Our sources for these vary, depending on the size of the trees we need, from bumpy chenille up through the various commercial brands. The biggest trees, however, are made of limbs cut from an artificial Christmas tree.

Early January is the best time to buy a plastic tree. If you're lucky, you might even find one being thrown out. A bolt cutter is the ideal tool for cutting through the heavy wire armature, but a hacksaw should also do the job.

A two-step pruning job is necessary to convert the branches from the cylindrical shape they come in to the cone-shaped trees you want to end up with. Don't get lazy and wind up with a pointed cylinder; carry the diagonal all the way down to the bottom branches. Leave about the bottom 1″ of the "trunk" bare for use in planting. Next, clumps of bristles have to be pruned to give the tree a natural, ragged look. We use a tin snips for this job.

You might want to make the branches upswept or downswept. You can get this effect simply by putting the tree in hot water and stroking it hard in the desired direction. You can see both effects in the color photo accompanying this article.

Before planting the trees we cover them with ground foam. To do this we mix several shades of dark green in different grinds (fine and medium) in a shoe box or other container. Then, in a plastic container large enough to immerse the entire tree, we dilute white glue about 50:50 with water (and a dash of rubbing alcohol or other wetting agent). Finally, we dip the tree in the diluted glue, shake off the excess, and then roll it in the foam.

To plant the trees, we drill holes in the scenery base (hardshell in our case) of a diameter just big enough to accept the wire trunk. Some members make up a batch of trees and plant them later. I prefer to plant each tree as soon as it's made, while still wet, so the wet glue can run down and bond the tree to the scenery. (Otherwise, use Hobsco Goo to secure the trees in place.) If the trees flop around, try to prop them up straight while the glue dries, although once the glue has dried you can bend the trunks of any you missed.

A popular saying among hobbyists is that nature often duplicates itself in miniature (weeds are little trees, pebbles can be used for scale boulders, and so on). Here's a case where humans follow that principle. The branches from an artificial Christmas tree can yield dozens of large pines in miniature. ✿

Jeff English

The holiday season past, our author attacks the branches of his Christmas tree with a bolt cutter.

Right. Branches fresh from the tree are cylindrical. **Far right.** They look like conifers once they're conical and roughed up a bit. John Nehrich photos.

Furnace filter forests

Black and white photos by Blair Amundson

An inexpensive way to make thousands of good-looking conifers

BY GAIL M. HOLLAND

WITHOUT doubt, mountain scenery is one of the most popular types of geographical terrain chosen by modelers to include on their layouts. While the plaster surface of the scenery is usually cleverly carved, colored, and disguised with dustings of foam or other litter, observation of various layouts indicates to me that often only cursory attention is given to another aspect of superdetailing of this type of scenery — trees. I do not mean that trees are not included. They are, but often in limited number. If we want a scene to really come alive, perhaps we should plant it abundantly with models of things that do live.

Residents of, and visitors to, our Canadian mountain areas will readily agree that a large portion of the panorama viewed from any given spot is taken up by forests. We don't want to recreate a model scene so dense that the railroad becomes secondary, but the end result should be the illusion of heavy forest growth, from the blending of the backdrop scenery to the edge of the benchwork, or perhaps even dropping down to floor level.

Articles have been published on various types of tree construction methods in the past years. One such successful method is that of inserting individual branches into predrilled holes in the trunk. While this method is salutary and realistic, it is readily evident that construction of whole forests (we are considering numbers in the thousands here) by this method would consume much of your railroading time. As well, it would exhaust your patience early on.

An inexpensive and faster way to produce very large numbers of realistic-appearing scale conifers is offered for your consideration. The method I'm going to describe represents a composite of the various techniques used by some of the Leth-bridge [Alberta, Canada] modelers, with refinements and modifications here and there. This is a relatively elementary method which you can learn quickly. Materials and tools needed are listed along with possible sources of supply. Finally, some planting suggestions, together with a few variations or enrichment ideas with the method are given.

TREE CONSTRUCTION

Step 1. Cutting trunk materials. Wood doweling, medical applicators, and toothpicks can be used for the tree trunks.

Cutting the doweling to specific lengths can be done easily if you take the time to prepare a simple trunk-measuring guide like the one shown in fig. 1. The length intervals should be 2 feet for small and medium trees, and 5 feet for trees 40 to 55 feet. Built into these measurements is an extra hidden 3-foot allowance for planting on the layout. Use a modeling saw to cut the doweling. It should be set on the guide so that only the length of the trunk desired is on the board, with the cutting done on the edge of the board.

Here's a suggestion that may save later frustration when you reach the planting step: When cutting a group of trunks in a particular session, cut a variety of different lengths from a bundle of dowels. Regardless of the degree of slope on which the planting is done, a variety of heights will be required. If you cut, construct, and plant large lots of one size only, the resulting effect will be something too uniform or monotonous. You will probably want to plant groups of trees as you make them and watch your scenery come alive, rather than wait until you have a large number ready. Therefore, if you have a variety of sizes ready in each lot you work on, planting will not have to wait. Two hundred trees will cover an incredibly small area. The scenery literally soaks them up once you begin.

It would be wise to hold off cutting the applicator-type trunks until after the pointing, scribing, and staining have been completed. These 40-scale-foot lengths (for HO scale) can then be cut into fairly equivalent lengths, such as 20-foot sizes, or 18- and 20-foot lengths. Perhaps you might prefer to save the applicators for the 30- or 35-foot lengths and reserve the leftover bits for second-growth trees, or distance-illusion foliage.

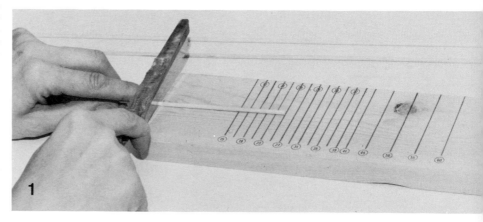

1

Step 2. Filing trunk tops. Doweling can be filed to a point with an inexpensive wood rasp. The rasp will dull soon, making work slower, so have another at hand. This step, manually done, is a bit tedious. If you own or have access to a horizontal disk-type sander, use it to speed up this step. Using a sander, I'm able to prepare several hundred trunks in an hour. When using the rasp, place the dowel at a slight angle to a flat wood surface and file toward a point away from you while slowly rotating the dowel.

The ¹⁄₁₆" applicators can be filed down far more quickly than the ⅛" doweling, which is one advantage of using them for trunks. File both ends of the applicators, as the smaller bits would be too difficult to grasp and file to a point after being cut.

Step 3. Staining trunk materials. I have prepared a suitable stain mixture using isopropyl alcohol and stain. I used the trial-and-error approach in an attempt to come close to the grayish-brown, bark-like color. No two batches have been precisely alike.

Stain and alcohol strengths should be at least 2:1, preferably 3:1 or more. Mix the ingredients in a container large enough to hold a batch of trunks. The length of time the trunks are left in the stain will depend on the strength as well as the particular colors used. Begin testing after about 20 minutes and keep checking periodically. When dry, the trunk color should be a silvered grayish brown. Allow the trunks to dry thoroughly before scribing.

Step 4. Scribing. Scribing adds textural highlights to the wooden trunks. Scribe the trunks using a razor saw. Lay the dowel on a flat surface, and while slowly rotating it, scrape away from you along the length of the trunk with long, even-pressured strokes of the teeth of your saw. Scribing produces a light-and-shadow effect by exposing some of the unstained inner surface of the wood. Much of the trunk will eventually be covered by foliage, but enough is visible so that it is worth taking the time to do this step.

Step 5. Preparation of the foliage. The main advantage of using the furnace filter medium for this method is that it can be trimmed nicely to the desired shape without disintegrating in the process. The preparation of the material involves only a few steps.

Begin by cutting the fiber into strips of various widths: ¼", ½", ¾", 1", and 1⅛", as shown in fig. 2. You will need at least three different sizes for each tree, depending on the height or the general form desired. Small to medium trees require ¼", ½", and 1" pieces, and the taller trees require a larger size for the base, as well as two or three smaller sizes for the upper branches. Cut each of the strips into at least two, but preferably three, layers, depending on the compactness of the filter you were able to obtain.

Next, cut the thin layers into squares. The reason for cutting different sizes is one of efficiency. You'll save considerable time at the shaping step. Also, the square layer pieces are easier to impale on the dowel trunk and are far easier to snip and shape, which is what gives the realistic look to the tree.

Step 6. Construction. The parts you have prepared are now ready to be assembled. Begin by placing the larger squares of filter on the dowel. Simply push the filter squares onto the pointed end of the dowel

2

3

4

and slide them toward the base. Two or three square layers of each size will usually be sufficient, but this will depend on the length of the trunk. See fig. 3. Avoid pushing the square layers too closely together. Carefully space them out right to the top, as the density will increase once the finishing foam is added. Hold the tree up to a light source to check on how much light is coming through the form.

Step 7. Shaping. The shaping of the tree begins by "destroying the block." Using a scissors, snip off the square corners and angles, working vertically, proceeding from bottom to top. Continue the shaping by randomly snipping bits away from each layer. Hold the tree at its base and rotate it as you snip. See fig. 3. Snip bits from both horizontal and vertical directions now. Most conifers are not symmetrical, and some are quite scraggly and sparse; therefore, don't hesitate to snip chunks from any section, or leave open bits in the middle or upper section. Be somewhat careful about snipping too much away from the top just yet, as a second slight trimming will be done after foam is applied and the adhesive dries.

The shaping process requires some practice. I suggest you refer to photographs of trees often until you catch on to it.

Scissors dull quite quickly when used for cutting furnace filters. Sharpen them occasionally for best efficiency. Different sizes of scissors should be used to accomplish different kinds of shaping effects.

Step 8. Applying adhesive. A number of readily available adhesives can be used. I used shellac because it is the least expensive adhesive for this process. Dip the trees directly into the can or pour the shellac in a rectangular container with a lid on it. Close the lid when not in use.

Hold the tree by the base and immerse the foliage area into the shellac. In the case of the longer trees, hold the tree in the middle with tweezers. Shake the tree slightly over the container to remove excess shellac. Then place the tree on an old kitchen cooling rack to allow the remaining excess shellac to drip off. Place another container under the rack to catch the drippings. I usually do only five to eight trees at a time, so that the shellac doesn't begin to set before I apply the foam.

Step 9. Applying foam. If you are able to obtain ground foam rubber in a good variety of shades, you will be able to forest your scenery with a wide range of subtle tints. You can do some mixing of closely related colors to add to this range. I have taken care in the foresting of the landscape with blended — yet distinctly different — shades of trees, similar, for instance, to the natural shades of white pine and spruce.

Pick up a tree by its base and hold it over the container of foam. With your other hand, begin scooping foam, a spoonful at a time and sprinkling it over the tree while you rotate it, as shown in fig. 4. Tap the top of the tree against the bowl of the spoon, so that the excess falls back into the container. You will have to sprinkle two or three spoonfuls over the tree to ensure that all foliage is covered. If you find the very tip of the tree a bit bare due to the shellac drying quickly, just dip the tip in the shellac again and reapply foam to only this section. After the foam has been applied, stick the trees in a Styrofoam sheet to dry.

I generally lightly spray a group of trees with 3M's Scotch Spra Mount to further secure the foam. Trees must dry completely before you attempt any final trimming, especially at the tops. As mentioned previously density increases when foam is applied. You will have to check for heavy patches of foliage and clip where needed to achieve just the right effect. You should now have a portion of the forest ready to plant.

PLANTING NOTES

Some planting cautions here may help produce a more pleasing finished scene. Generally, holes can be made in plaster scenery with a smooth awl. Push the awl gently into the plaster just the few scale feet required to hold the trunk securely. Using an awl rather than a drill prevents the breaking off of bits of plaster and exposing the white plaster beneath the surface and around the hole. A threaded awl can be used to penetrate harder types of scenery. Be very cautious about making large numbers of holes at once. Make one or two at a time; plant a few trees; then stand back and judge their placement in relation to the rest of the foliage before

Bill of materials

Trunks

Birch doweling, 1/8" diameter. Obtainable from lumber outlets and many hobby suppliers

Medical applicators, 1/16" diameter, 6" lengths. May be purchased in small packages from drugstores or large lots from medical supply firms

Flat wood toothpicks

Round wood cocktail toothpicks

Isopropyl alcohol

Nongrain-raising type of wood stain. Available at many paint dealers in a color range including oak, mahogany, walnut, teak, brown, and black

Foliage

Furnace filter or "filter media." This must be the plant fiber (cellulose) type of media, about 1" thickness. It must be fairly compact and not too airy. Available in pre-cut sizes or 4-foot width rolls. Green-colored filter material is best. Possible suppliers: hardware outlets, sheet metal firms, heating and furnace suppliers or contractors, and possibly refrigeration suppliers. [For a local supplier check your Yellow Pages under "Filtering Materials & Supplies" and "Filters — Air & Gas."]

Adhesives

White shellac used full strength

3M's Scotch Spra Mount adhesive

Pliobond

Finishing Material

Finely ground foam rubber. Woodland Scenics, Elm City, or Architectural Scale Models, Inc.

Dolomite. (For a snow scene.) Obtainable from building supply contractors

Water putty

Tools

Razor saw for cutting and scribing doweling

Tongs or long tweezers

Wood rasps

Trunk-measuring guide

Horizontal disk sander (optional)

Heavy-duty shears or tin snips

Variety of scissors, including blunt-end primary type, fabric, household types, and heavy fabric shears

Small kitchen cooling rack

Plastic rectangular container with lid

Containers for architectural foam

Teaspoons

Smooth-tipped and threaded awls

Syringe with curved spout

A furnace filter forest. You can create an impressive-looking forest like this one following the method described by the author. This scene on Jim Noble's Monashee Western Ry. shows some of the thousands of trees on this layout.

continuing with more planting. Otherwise, the finished slope will appear to be planted in the neat, uniform, planned rows of the Forestry Service, rather than the random growth that appears naturally.

I have found Pliobond to be better than the brittle white glues for planting trees. It dries slowly and continues to be slightly tacky. This allows you to adjust the placement angle of the trees if necessary. Using a syringe, place several drops of Pliobond in the hole and set in the tree. Pack small bits of loose foam around the base of the trunk to cover up the hole made for the tree. This foam will serve as forest ground cover. Water putty can be used to add root systems to random trees in the immediate foreground.

The exact spacing of the trees will depend on the effect you wish to create on a particular part of your scenery, be it sparse, dense, or a mass-planting effect.

A mass-planting technique allows you to densely cover an area without expending as much time in construction as would first appear. Mass planting is best attempted on a fairly well-defined slope. Choose trunks of ¹⁄₁₆″ diameter and about 30 scale feet in height. Follow the steps through as previously given, but cover only the top third of the trunk with foliage. Plant the trees

¾″ apart. You may leave the timber stand with the trunks exposed in an area adjacent to a logged-out area, or you may disguise all of the trunks by surrounding the perimeter of a mass-planting area with enough trees foliaged the entire height. Jim Noble has used this subtlety to camouflage an access hatchway on his Monashee Western and blend it into the surrounding area of the whole slope, giving the impression of uninterrupted density.

While this article does not cover the construction of deciduous trees, they should be interspersed with the conifers. They should be more numerous on the lower slopes.

Often seen in a mass of trees are single dead trees or small areas of them. They appear grayish from a distance and can be simulated by giving the trees a more thorough clipping before applying gray colored foam over the sparse foliage. This will appear as dead branches in the mass.

Diseased timber, with some of its foliage fairly intact, often has a rusty appearance. This can be duplicated by a more thorough clipping of the filter medium before applying rust-colored shades of foam. Plant such trees sparingly, keeping the effect subtle.

You may use those trunk stubs mentioned earlier, as well as flat toothpicks, to build the type of trees needed to blend the

flat backdrop with the three-dimensional scenery. This will add to the illusion of depth and distance. Dip some of these 1″ to 1½″ stubs in shellac, then into a medium-size grade of foam. Let them dry; then re-dip them in shellac and foam once more. No furnace filter medium is required for these trees. The foam alone is sufficient.

Use bluish-green shades of foam for these trees, as you are trying to duplicate the haze-like quality of objects seen at a distance. These stubs are glued on the backdrop and just barely touch the scenery at the base. They must blend into the flat backdrop as well as the area immediately in front of them.

The next grouping of trees from the backdrop may consist of trees made from the flat toothpicks. Save your snippets from the shaping of the larger trees and use them to make this type of tree. Use the same layer and shaping method as with the other trees, but on a much smaller scale. You can turn this type of smaller-growth trees into "half" trees by trimming away most of the back after the adhesive has dried. This will allow them to rest comfortably against the stubs on the scenery. Again, use bluish-green shades of foam for these trees.

Second-growth trees can be constructed from doweling stubs or the round toothpicks cut in half. They should be about an inch high. Since the toothpicks are already pointed, this step is sidestepped. You need only stain them and scribe them very lightly before cutting them in half. Use very small bits of filter layers for foliage. After placing the filter on the trunk, dip the small trees in shellac and allow them to dry completely before shaping; otherwise, the furnace filter falls off the trunks. Dip them in shellac again, cover with foam, and give them a final clipping.

Plant these second-growth trees in an area that was perhaps logged out and has now been given over to planned reforestation. Also, they may be used for a timber-replacement site — where timber had been cut to make way for a bridge, trestle, industrial situation, etc.

Interested in modeling a snow-covered forest? A substance that I've found to be ideal for simulating snow is one by the trade name of Dolomite. It is of just the right-size granule, crystaline shape, and sparkle to be quite effective. It should be applied after the trees have been firmly planted. Spray the area you wish to be snow-covered with 3M's Scotch Spra Mount adhesive and then slowly sprinkle the Dolomite directly over the trees from a height of 5 or 6″. Some of the Dolomite will be caught by the foliage itself and some will sift through the branches to act as even cover on the forest floor. Be careful not to build up too heavy a layer on the higher slopes as they should appear to be somewhat windswept just at the edge of the timberline. Dolomite is a calcium magnesium carbonate compound often used in the production of high-grade lime.

You will find that with a bit of practice the stages in the making of furnace filter forests will be easily mastered. You can then utilize small blocks of time to work on one or more of these stages so that you will have some trees at each step of the process always in readiness. ✿

Deciduous anyone?

Malcolm Furlow's technique for making large, broadleaf trees

BY BILLY HAYNES
PHOTOS BY MALCOLM FURLOW

MALCOLM FURLOW'S layouts have always featured great evergreen trees made with balsa trunks and caspia foliage. [He described the technique in the April 1984 MR.] Recently, however, he's been working more with deciduous trees (those that shed their leaves). He and his cohorts make these by cementing sugar bush branches to broomweed trunks. More about that later.

Malcolm says that in the past "I sort of steered away from deciduous trees because I find the 'tried-and-true' materials unacceptable. Lichen, sawdust, foam, wire, mesh, and those God-awful square computer card punch-outs — all that artificial stuff looks so fake to me. It looks blobby and lifeless."

He started looking around in nature for tree material. As he says, "Mother Nature is constantly repeating and reproducing herself on different scales. The shape and form of a large tree can be found in a small bush. It was in dead brush that I could most easily decipher the trunk and branch patterns of a large tree duplicated. The choices for realistic tree trunks were practically infinite. They were in the creek right outside my door.

"My favorite trunk and branch systems, however, I found in fields and pastures

The large tree, left, and the yellow tree behind the engine are prime examples of trees made using Malcolm Furlow's technique. The scene was shot on Malcolm's Sn3 Koester's Canyon diorama.

Left. Step one in making a deciduous tree is trimming the dried weed tru[nk]. Broomweed and sagebrush work well. Most modelers can probably find go[od]

out in the country. It's called broomweed and is easily spotted under and around fence lines. Ranchers and farmers have no use for it, and neither do livestock. Here in Texas the stuff is everywhere and usually stands about 1 to 2 feet tall. In some areas, I think sage would work well also."

So much for trunks and primary branches, then. Finding a suitable foliage was another matter. At a nearby wholesale florist outlet Malcolm discovered sugar bush, a material florists often use to fill out flower arrangements. It comes dried, manicured, and nicely packaged. Sometimes you can also find it in art and craft stores. Sugar bush comes in many colors, but the handiest for model trees is the undyed straw yellow. You can paint it any color you want.

Malcolm has found it particularly effective for modeling in the larger scales: "Sugar bush, as a leaf material, has a great broadleaf pattern. It might be considered a tad large for HO scale, but it works. It's ideal for S, O, and LGB. I've been presently working in these larger scale formats and making deciduous trees with trunks ranging from 6" to 18" high.

These trees have great see-through qualities. Malcolm says "They add a great deal of verticality which, to me, is the basic ingredient in diorama and miniature scenery of any kind. I like to get a lot going on the up and down. Trees also provide a nice three-dimensional feel to the modeling, especially when lit for photographic purposes. They cast good shadows."

Furlow thinks that deciduous trees, like evergreens, look better on a layout when grouped, usually in odd-numbered lots of three or five. Mixing different heights also works well. And, of course, scattered singles, when appropriate, are okay. But the general idea with tree placement is to establish a random pattern so they don't appear to have been planted by a landscaping firm.

Another nice feature of deciduous trees is that, unlike evergreens, they can be painted in a variety of colors, depending on the season of the year portrayed in the layout.

Tree wizards at work. Author Haynes, left, and Malcolm Furlow paint trees, using spray cans.

MAKING A TREE

It's best to make these trees outdoors, as you'll be using cyanoacrylate adhesive and spray paint, and neither is good for your eyes and lungs. If you must work indoors use a fan, work in a paint spray booth, or provide otherwise for good ventilation.

You'll need the following items: weed tree trunks, sugar bush branch material, scissors, ACC, ACC accelerator, and spray paint.

To make a tree, first take one of your weed trunks and trim it until it looks right to you. Poke the trimmed trunk into a piece of 1"- or 2"-thick Styrofoam so that it is free standing and easily accessible for adding the smaller branches.

Snip the individual branches away from the trunk of the sugar bush and trim them. Lay out a dozen or so branch

and leaf clusters that look like they'll do the trick.

Hold a sugar bush branch where you want it against the lower part of the main trunk and apply a few drops of ACC. We use Hot Stuff. Spray the glue joint with the accelerator (Hot Shot) and it'll set up in a second or two, enabling you to work quickly. Keep adding branches, working your way up the tree.

If painting is desired, paint the trunk first with short spurts of Pactra Light Earth (or whatever suits you) while rotating it. Spray mostly from the bottom up.

Next spray the foliage from the side and underneath with a dark green. We use Pactra's Forest Green in a spray can. Highlight the tree with a lighter green (Pactra's Chromate Green is our choice) sprayed from above.

That's it. Let the trees dry a day or two, then plant 'em and enjoy. ۵

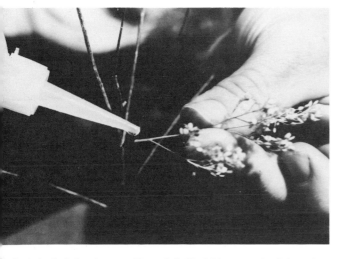

ivalents in their local areas. **Above left.** Next trim sugar bush branches in their trunk. These will become the foliage. **Above.** Use ACC to cement the leafy branches to the limbs. **Above.** A squirt of ACC accelerator and the branch will be attached. Add more branches, working from the bottom up.

Evergreens everywhere

An easy way to make lots of pine trees inexpensively

BY BRIAN HOLTZ
PHOTOS BY JIM HEDIGER

FOR some time I have wrestled with the problem of providing large quantities of pine or spruce trees to fill the background areas of my mountainous layout. In many mountainous areas, the hillsides are literally covered with such trees. While there are a number of very nice trees available, their cost or the time required to make them limits their use to closeup foreground locations.

The answer came from the wife of a friend, who suggested using bumpy green chenille from the local craft shop. I followed her advice and bought a 9-yard package of the bumpy chenille. By the time they were all finished, I had made 320 evergreens ¾" to 1" high from the $1.29 package of chenille.

The bumpy chenille trees are quite similar to the brush-bristle type of tree, except the fibers are softer and the trunk is more flexible. The roll of chenille is cut into short pieces as shown in fig. 1. By trimming a little off the top, the shape can be changed somewhat to get a little variety. It's a simple job that one can work on while watching tv with the family.

The trees are acceptable as they are, but much better-looking trees can be made by spray-painting them to hide the wire armature and give them a more realistic color. Blue spruce trees can be made by spraying the finished product with a shot of dark blue spray paint. Color is a personal preference, so one may want to use different shades to have the trees blend into the existing scenery or to provide contrast as I have done in my snow scene. I use the least expensive large cans of spray paint from the discount stores and the results are en-

tirely satisfactory. Flat colors look the best, but even a slight gloss is not objectionable.

To paint the trees, I affix them to a board so the force of the spray will not send them rolling away. I use a Styrofoam board with a series of small holes punched into its surface with an awl. A drop of glue is then used to hold the trees in the holes: fig. 2. When it sets up, the trees are spray-painted as shown in fig. 3. The whole batch is then set aside to dry. After painting, I carry the whole Styrofoam piece to the layout area and pull the trees off as I plant them. The glue used to hold the trees for painting serves as a nice firm base when they are planted. A small hole in the scenery and another drop of glue take care of the planting job.

Bumpy chenille is also available in larger sizes. One size allows me to make a

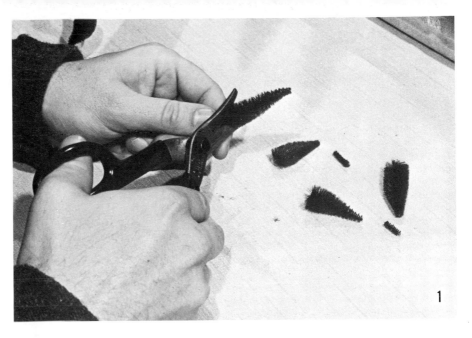

1

3½" tree and a 1" tree out of each bump; however, this size is slightly more expensive. The larger trees need some additional treatment to look right, so I do some pruning, fig. 4, to reduce the symmetrical appearance and uniform shape. These large trees are painted by holding the very bottom of the tree with an old glove and spraying the foliage areas. While they are wet, I shake on Boyd's scenic grass to improve the texture and add additional green and brown colors.

The large unpruned trees can also be used as armatures for adding ground foam foliage. I have found the larger foam sizes look best because the fine material tends to fill in and make the tree too symmetrical. A mixture of colors and sizes of ground foam looks the best.

The chenille trees can be made in a nice variety of sizes, so it is easy to use several different sizes together. This increases the realism, since most modelers tend to use the same-size trees throughout. I plant the evergreens in odd-numbered groups (for some reason it looks better) and make sure the tops of the trees point skyward. One nice thing about these trees is that they can be planted on a hillside, allowed to dry, and then they can be bent to a vertical position.

Multiple sizes of chenille trees have also enabled me to make use of forced perspective. Placing the smallest trees in the most distant part of the scene adds a lot of depth. I was surprised at how easy and effective this forced perspective can be accomplished.

2

3

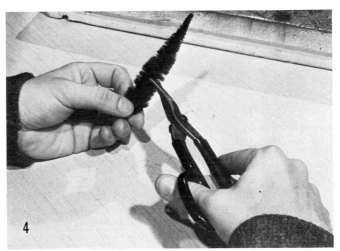

4

Fig. 1. The RPI club used the flat trees described here to suggest three-dimensional trees growing in the 2″ space between the buildings and the backdrop.

Flat background trees

Solving a common scenery problem with trees that look three-dimensional but are less than ½″ thick

BY JOHN NEHRICH
PHOTOS BY THE AUTHOR

ONCE upon a time, so the story goes, a director of the mighty Pennsylvania RR made a sneering remark about a short line. "Well," said that short line's president, "our railroad may not be as long as yours, but the track is just as wide."

The same might be said of modern walkaround layouts with continuous backdrops. Whether they're club-sized or 4 x 8s with a backdrop down the middle, they're all just as wide. In any one spot the scene is probably only 2 to 3 feet deep, and a lot of the scenery effort must go into hiding the boundary between the three-dimensional scenery and the two-dimensional backdrop.

Figure 1 shows an area where our Rensselaer Polytechnic Institute club solved a fairly typical scenery problem at the town of Regis on our New England, Berkshire & Western RR. Regis is based on the real-life town of North Creek, N. Y. In North Creek, the state highway roughly parallels the tracks at a distance of several hundred feet. At trackside you see the backs of the buildings that line the near side of the highway, but you can barely make out the highway itself.

On our layout the highway ended up right along the backdrop, and due to space limitations, it's only ½″ wide. Fine so far, but when we added standard, three-dimensional trees along the road, they gave too much shade. On the prototype you look past the buildings to sun-drenched areas beyond. What we needed were flat trees for our narrow road. Woodland Scenics tree kits provided the answer, as illustrated in fig. 2.

MAKING FLAT TREES

You might make a regular three-dimensional tree and press it between two brick bats, but we think we have a better way. We use the Woodland Scenics cast-metal tree trunks flat, just the way they come out of the box. See fig. 3. We paint one side a brownish-gray, using a mixture of Floquil's Reefer Gray and Roof Brown.

Next we cut a roughly circular shape from the foliage net, making sure this patch is bigger than the spread of the branches. We keep the foliage net flat and don't stretch it.

After applying Walthers Goo generously to the unpainted backs of the branches, we press the trunk down into the foliage, as shown in fig. 4. Then we stretch some of the leftover foliage and glue it in front of the branches. This will partially obscure the limbs and give a see-through look to the tree, yet we'll have a solid wall of green in front of the backdrop. A finished flat tree is shown in fig. 5.

INSTALLATION

Before installing the flat trees on the layout, we glue pieces of foliage net to the bottom of the backdrop up to the height of the lower branches.

The scenic effect you want will determine how you treat the backdrop and group the flat trees. If you want only a few prominent trees, you probably should add even more unstretched foliage to the backdrop, bringing it up almost as high as the tops of the flat trees. If you want a dense woods, overlap the trees; then stretch some foliage across the trunks to partially obscure them too. For in-town locations we've had good success with cementing pictures of buildings to the backdrop, using the flat trees to frame them and hide the fact they are two-dimensional.

Sometimes it pays to be contrary. Most modelers reserve Woodland Scenics trees for the foreground, using weeds and lichen for a mass foliage effect in the background. On the NEB&W we've been doing just the opposite, and in the end, it's results that count. ▢

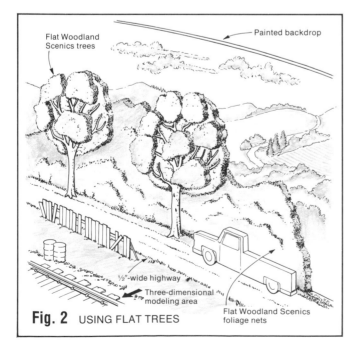

Flat Woodland Scenics trees

Painted backdrop

½″-wide highway

Three-dimensional modeling area

Flat Woodland Scenics foliage nets

Fig. 2 USING FLAT TREES

Fig. 3. The club uses the Woodland Scenics tree trunks flat, just as they come out of the box.

Fig. 4. The front half is painted, then the trunk is glued to a patch of unstretched foliage material.

Fig. 5. Foliage material is teased and cemented to the trunk so limbs show through in places.

The appearance of standing individual blades of grass is highly realistic.

Zap-texturing for foliage

An early scientific discovery can be applied to produce excellent foliage effects

BY D. DEREK VERNER

MODEL scenery construction has come a long way since the early days of the hobby. Hardshell, zip texturing, the use of ground foam, and latex rock molds are only a few of the many methods that have been developed to enable us to create an amazingly realistic stage upon which our prized locomotives and rolling stock may perform.

Zip texturing, as described in the Kalmbach softcover book SCENERY FOR MODEL RAILROADS has made it possible for even the most inexperienced modeler to create large areas of realistic textures quickly and easily. However, under conditions of close scrutiny, zip texturing fails to hold up when it is used to simulate grass. Dyed sawdust, flock, or ground foam sprinkled onto a glue-covered surface do not fare much better. The flock looks pretty good, but its fibers land in a haphazard manner that often fails to capture the sense of individual blades of grass growing from the soil. A commercial flock handgun helps somewhat, since its airstream tends to cause the fibers to align themselves like miniature javelins, but the results are still disappointing. We need some method to make the fibers stand up like iron filings under the influence of a magnet.

Fortunately, the process that will do this job has existed for several thousand years. The same static electricity that we encounter on a dry winter day (when we touch a grounded object after walking across a rug) can be utilized to plant very realistic-looking grass. The forces of attraction and repulsion that form a field around electrically charged bodies are utilized to stand the fibers on end as they are applied. Because this process uses electricity, and in honor of Linn Westcott's origination of zip-texturing, I have elected to call this electrostatic application process "zap-texturing."

Zap-texturing requires the use of an applicator and a high-voltage power supply, which allows the particles or fibers to be charged to a high potential. This high-potential charge causes the fibers to repel each other and be attracted to the surface being textured. For our purposes, a Wimshurst Electrostatic Machine (available from Edmund Scientific Co.,) will produce all the high voltage needed. Under ideal conditions (a dry day), a Wimshurst Machine is capable of producing up to 75,000 volts, but it cannot produce more than a few billionths of an ampere. Thus, while it can pack a painful wallop, it is not dangerous to most people. [Anyone with a heart condition or a pace-maker should use extreme caution to guard against any possible shock.] For most people, the shock is harmless, but the startle reaction might cause some degree of personal injury. The startle reaction may also cause one to throw the equipment across the room — a situation that could lead to premature failure of the unit.

As the Wimshurst Electrostatic Machine comes from the manufacturer, it has a crank handle that must be turned continuously during use. It is a simple matter to replace the hand crank with some method of turning the machine with a motor. Figure 1 shows the original machine and fig. 2 shows how I motorized mine. I replaced the crank with a short length of $\frac{3}{16}$" rod that is slotted at one end. The other end is connected to a geared down d.c. motor which turns at about 60 rpm. Both of the jingle bells that come on the unit were discarded and replaced with a pair of wing nuts to facilitate connections at the high-voltage terminals.

The applicator is made from a 3"- or 4"- diameter plastic jar as shown in fig. 3. I used a length of automobile ignition cable for the connecting wire. Note that this must be the normal type of cable as the noise-suppression type will not work. A ½"-wide strip of aluminum foil is cemented to the inside of the jar about 1" down from the top. Another strip of the roll is cemented to the inside of the jar from the ring, down the side, and across

Fig. 1

Fig. 2

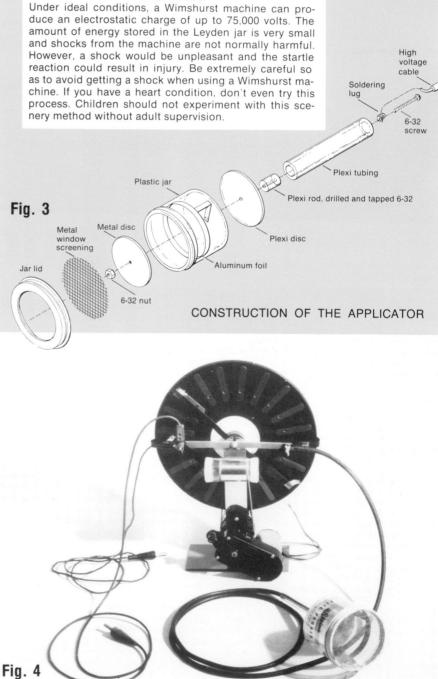

Fig. 3

High voltage cable

Soldering lug

6-32 screw

Plexi tubing

Plexi rod, drilled and tapped 6-32

Plastic jar

Plexi disc

Aluminum foil

Metal disc

Metal window screening

6-32 nut

Jar lid

CONSTRUCTION OF THE APPLICATOR

Fig. 4

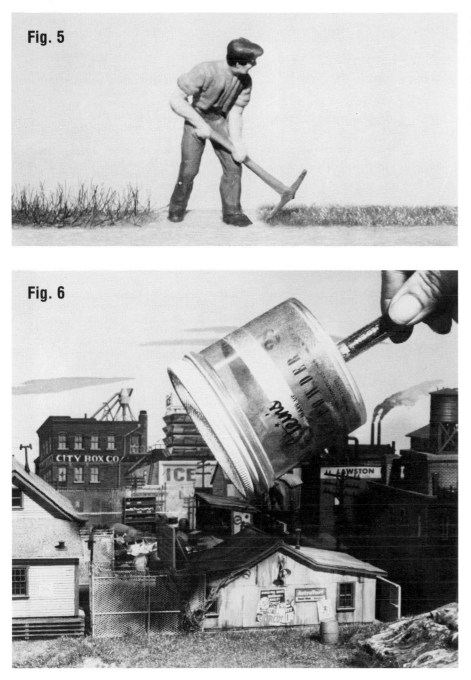

Fig. 5

Fig. 6

the bottom of the jar. This strip serves as a conductor to carry the electrical charge to the fibers even when there is only a small amount of them in the jar.

I also made a smaller jar out of a medicine vial that is interchangeable with the big jar. This smaller applicator is used to apply grass in areas near buildings or in restricted spaces where the big applicator will not fit. The free end of the cable is equipped with a spade lug so it can be connected to the high-voltage source as shown in fig. 4.

There are several types and lengths of commercial flock available. Most craft shops carry the short nylon fibers shown on the right in fig. 5. I use several shades of green, one yellow, and one brown, blending these in varying proportions to obtain realistic colors. First-hand observation of grass will show there is a wide variety of colors present. Fibers of this short variety are suitable for closely cropped lawns in HO scale. The longer type of flock, seen in the left portion of fig. 5, is available from Boyd, Terra-Tex, and other model railroad suppliers. This length is suitable for fields and meadows since it is about ankle high in HO scale. Random lengths of nylon or wool yarn may be cut with a sharp scissors and used alone or mixed with flock. Just comb out a length of suitably colored yarn and clip off short lengths.

The area to be textured is first painted to represent an earth color so any loss of texturing will not reveal white plaster. Use white glue or matte medium as an adhesive for the fibers. To attract the fibers, the glue must be well grounded. This is easily accomplished by sticking a pin into the wet adhesive and connecting a wire from the grounded side of the Wimshurst machine. The applicator, filled with fibers, is connected to the opposite terminal.

To apply the fibers, turn on the Wimshurst machine and hold the applicator by its plastic insulated handle. Bring the applicator over the adhesive area and gently roll the applicator back and forth between your fingers to help release the fibers. See figure 6. The fibers will leap from the applicator and

How Zap-texturing works

The applicator containing the fiber is charged to a high negative potential. (The process works well whether the applicator is positive or negative with respect to ground). When it is brought close to the glue-covered and grounded surface, like charges repel and electrons are forced away from the area immediately under the applicator. This leaves the area with an induced positive charge. Since unlike charges attract, the positively charged area draws the negatively charged particles of fiber from the applicator.

As soon as they arrive, however, they lose their negative charge and gain a positive charge. Since they now possess a charge similar to the surface and to the other particles, they are repelled and attempt to return to the applicator. The glue holds them fast.

When the applicator is removed, the area returns to a neutral state because of the ground connection. Sweeping the applicator very close to the surface repeats the induction process and greatly increases the electrostatic forces. Those particles that are not firmly attached *do* jump back to the applicator.

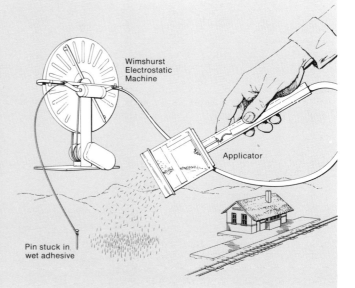

Wimshurst Electrostatic Machine

Applicator

Pin stuck in wet adhesive

imbed themselves in the adhesive. Every once in a while, hold the top of the applicator close to the surface and sweep it back and forth. This will cause the imbedded fibers to stand up straight, and any unattached ones will be attracted back to the applicator. Continue this application process until the required grass density is obtained. Afterward, be sure to let the surface dry, undisturbed, until the adhesive is thoroughly set.

WARNING: A high voltage charge remains in the applicator even after the power is turned off. Do not touch any portion of the applicator except the plastic handle until the high voltage terminal has been shorted to ground by means of a well-insulated conductor that discharges the capacitor built into the Wimshurst machine.

After the adhesive has set and dried completely, I vacuum up any loose fibers that are left on the surface. I use a piece of nylon hosiery, inserted in the neck of the vacuum and held in place with a rubber band, to recover the loose fibers so they can be reused later on.

The principles of zap-texturing are also useful for adding foliage to trees. The short nylon flock can be applied to "bottle brush" evergreen trees to add some realistic needles on the branches. Figure 7 shows the results of one such application. I use a pair of scissors to trim the tree first and remove some of its unrealistic symmetry. Coat the bristles with some artist's spray adhesive until the tree is wet. Attach the ground lead to the trunk and apply the fibers in the same way that the grass is applied.

Deciduous trees for foreground use can also be created using the zap texturing method of foliage application. Form the trunk and branches from ordinary stranded, tinned hook-up wire obtained from your local electronics supplier. Cut a number of pieces that are long enough to reach from the roots to the end of the longest branches (about 8″ in HO scale). Remove the insulation and bundle them together to form the trunk of the tree. Do not twist them together; instead, bind them tightly with string or wire and solder the trunk together between the bindings. Use a torch or heavy iron and a lot of solder. Remove the bindings and finish the soldering of the trunk.

Next, bend the upper ends of the branches away from the trunk as shown in fig. 8. The large branches are done by grouping several strands together in the same manner that was used for the trunk.

Figure 9 shows the step-by-step process that is used to make smaller trees. Note that the smaller branches have been pinched to give them an angular look that more closely approximates real tree branches. All of the multiwire branches should be soldered at this time to give them more body and stiffness. Be sure to leave one long wire extending downward so the tree can be planted later on. Remove all traces of the soldering flux by boiling the tree armature in dishwashing detergent.

The next step in making the deciduous tree is to coat the trunk and branches with modeling paste as shown in fig. 10. Fill in the gaps and voids in the trunk and brush the paste on in the direction of the tips of the branches. The idea is to make the branches taper toward the ends as they do on a real tree. Use a stiff, coarse-bristled brush to create a bark-like texture on the surface. After you have allowed it to dry overnight, the tree is ready for painting.

Most model trees are painted in colors that are too brown. The best way to obtain a realistic color is to go outdoors and look at a real tree. The actual color is closer to gray than it is to brown. Since these model trees have so many branches, I paint the entire tree with a base color using an air-brush. When this dries, it is easy to go back and dry-brush the trunk and main branches with a lighter mixture of the base color. This dry-brushing will accentuate the bark texture.

Now, hook up the Wimshurst machine and apply long fiber flock to the tree. This represents the myriad tiny branches that are too numerous to model by any other means. The adhesive (thinned white glue or matte medium) should be brushed only on the fine outer tips of the branches. Allow the fibers to dry thoroughly and then lightly mist them with some of the tree's base color.

Next, use the applicator to apply Woodland Scenics green ground foam. Use a spray adhesive for this and spray it on so it hits only the tips of the branches. Try to keep the adhesive off all of the thicker branches. The ground foam is a bit heavier than the flock, so it may take a bit more agitation to get it to move out of the applicator.

Also, since the electrostatic charge is not of an even intensity over the entire surface of the tree, it tends to concentrate at the sharp points. Thus, the foam is naturally attracted to the tips of the fibers, resulting in the most realistic effect, shown in fig. 11. Other leaf materials, such as check punchings or fine confetti, may also be applied in the same manner.

Don't limit your use of zap-texturing to grass and trees. There are a number of other places where the technique can be of use. Why not be a big spender and equip all of your miniature ladies with nice fur coats? Experiment is the name of the game, and let's hope you are pleasantly surprised (let's not say "shocked") by the results.

Water and how to model it

Methods used on the NEB&W

BY JOHN NEHRICH
PHOTOS BY THE AUTHOR

YOUNGSTERS, when drawing a picture of a lake, invariably reach for a blue crayon. We modelers, who have learned the hard way that grass is olive-colored, not emerald green, that tree trunks are more gray than brown, and that bricks are more brown than red, may chuckle at these young artists. "Water isn't blue," we say, holding up a glass of water.

So what color *is* water? Or more to the point: *What color do we see when we look at water?*

That's a trick question, of course. There is no one right answer, because each body of water is different, and the same body of water looks different under varying conditions. There are a number of factors that account for what we perceive to be the color of water.

● Dissolved minerals affect the color. The more concentrated the minerals, the darker the water. By analogy, a cup of coffee gets darker the longer it is brewed, though it remains transparent. Generally speaking, though, minerals do not significantly color most large bodies of water.

● Materials in suspension (mud or algae, for example) both color and lighten the water. To extend the coffee analogy, adding milk to coffee makes it lighter. Suspensions also make water translucent, or even opaque, reducing transparency.

● Air bubbles (aeration) caused by water passing over falls and rapids, or by wind or wave action stirring up the surface, are large enough to scatter light, but they don't color the water. Pour a glass of HOT water, and watch it go from cloudy to clear as the bubbles get a chance to surface.

● Reflections of objects on the surface of the water affect our perception of its color also. A still body of water gives a mirror-like reproduction of its surroundings, especially the blue of the sky overhead. When the surface is disturbed with ripples or waves, each portion of the wave is angled slightly different, so the scene is broken up. On individual waves we may also be seeing a reflection of the sky, the sparkle of the sun's reflection, and an image of the distant shoreline.

● The viewer's position, relative to the sun, also plays a role. If we look at water with the sun directly in front of us, we see mainly glare. With the sun over our shoulder the same water takes on the color of the sky, the shoreline, and whatever minerals or materials are in the water. Also, the angle from which we look at the water makes a difference. When we look straight down into shallow water we can see the bottom, but when we look across a body of water we see almost total reflection.

MODELING WATER

Before you begin to model water on your layout, you need to determine what kind of water the scene calls for: deep, shallow, clear, muddy, still, rippled. Then find a photograph that best approximates the type of water, weather and lighting conditions, and viewing angle that you're looking for, and then copy that.

Much of the water on our New England, Berkshire & Western is polyester, a liquid which (when a catalyst is added) hardens to a clear, flat surface. It can, however, be colored by adding tints. The chief advantages of polyester are that it can duplicate the glossy rippled effect of the prototype's surface and that it can be colored to match the prototype effect you're after. Its chief disadvantage is that it stinks, a factor that you need to consider if your layout is in an area where other humans reside.

If you are modeling clear, shallow water where you want the bottom to show, you can get by with modeling the bottom and pouring uncolored polyester to the desired scale depth. This is practical only when the water is less than an HO scale 4 to 5 feet deep, i.e. approximately ½" or less.

Crystal clear water is not all that common in nature, however, and it has limited applications on most layouts. So how do we model deeper water? We could model it to exact scale, as with shallow water, but this would involve many gallons of polyester — an impractical approach. A better approach that will achieve the same effect is to decrease the depth and increase the color concentration. Even a ½"-thick layer can be colored sufficiently, especially if we make a flat, featureless bottom. But don't grab the polyester yet.

If you look at the accompanying photo of the Hudson River (above right), you can see that the reflection of the blue

Left. The milk train accelerates out of Chateaugay at Hastings Bay, with its profitable cargo. Bill McChesney's redetailed and painted Gem-10 Wheeler provides the power. The author describes the techniques used for modeling the water here and at other places on the RPI Club's layout. **Above.** This photo of the Hudson River at Troy, N. Y., illustrates how the reflection of both sky and shoreline, as well ripples, affects our perception of the color of water.

sky is the predominant effect. The reason this is so is that the sky is a very strong half-hemisphere source of light. That being the case, it often negates the other factors that give water its apparent color.

Without extending our backdrop up across the ceiling and making it translucent and strongly backlit, we can't hope to simulate this strong half-hemisphere source of light. Therefore, we must compensate by introducing some blue into the model water.

In the Regis scene, the effect we were after was of shallow water with the bottom visible; therefore, we added *no* blue. But in the Red Rocks scene most of the water is deep, with only a thin margin along some of the fill where you should be able to see down to the bottom. Here we needed a deep blue.

SPECIFIC EXAMPLES

The four model scenes that accompany this article (Hastings Bay is shown twice) were all photographed on the NEB&W, the Rennselaer Polytechnic Institute Model Railroad Club's layout.

Although polyester is our standard medium for modeling water, this method requires that all of the shoreline and any underwater scenery be in place before adding polyester. In a couple of locations we had to use temporary means to allow the scene to look finished in the photograph, which in this article will let us compare the effects.

SOUTH RIVER

So that we could include a photo of this unfinished area in a slide clinic, and since we didn't have time to use polyester, we

Here we see Bob Latham's Ten-Wheeler no. 250 at the head of the "tin-can," the Barrington to Chateaugay local freight, as it crosses the mouth of the South River. The real water in the riverbed, temporarily poured there for this photograph, just doesn't look real. It's too transparent and too flat.

John Nehrich and Jeff English

More temporary water is featured in this scene at Red Rocks as Rutland-detailed USRA light Mikado (modified and painted by Bill McChesney) leads the way for a northbound freight. The brush-mark-rippled water is semigloss paint; it looks good in photos but the author says it's unconvincing in person.

used real water. The lack of any sky reflection and the absolute flatness of the water is what spoils the effect. Under unusual conditions, it is possible to have a lake as smooth as glass, but it makes the model scene look fake, even though in this case the water is the real thing.

RED ROCKS

The realistic water in this scene is a fluke. Because only half of the scene is finished, we've put off casting the water. While waiting for the scenery to catch up, we painted the chipboard river bottom with a dark blue semigloss paint, just to provide a feel of water to the scene. (The ripples you see are just brush marks and were not intentional.) While this is an easy modeling technique that looks surprisingly realistic in photographs, when seen in person the water imparts no feeling of depth; it is totally opaque.

Now that the rest of the scene is nearly finished, we face the prospect of casting the water with the grim but distinct possibility that our finished product may not be as effective — in photos, at least — as our temporary measure. Our current thought is to repaint the chipboard a darker color, but lighten it to a sandy brown as it reaches the shore along the fills. Champlain Blue tint would be mixed into the ¼"-deep polyester.

Compared to the real water at South River, this scene demonstrates the value of color and of a glossy-rippled surface, even if at the expense of transparency.

REGIS

The river at Regis is an example of the use of clear polyester, especially appropriate for shallow water. We painted the cat-box litter on the creek bottom slightly darker than litter in its natural state. Note the rippled effect under the bridge; the property of polyester that puts it at the head of the class is this tendency to ripple as it sets up.

HASTINGS BAY

Some of the techniques we came up with for coloring the polyester were born of desperation, in the heat of the pour. Polyester has to be poured in thin layers. If poured too thick and with too much catalyst, it can crack from the heat generated by the exothermic reaction. All of the polyester should be colored first and then the catalyst added to each batch about to be poured. We made the mistake of adding catalyst first, and then coloring. Our first batch was dyed a deep blue, with "pearl essence" added to make it somewhat transparent. The pearl essence is a strange substance, and its effect is hard to describe, but it *didn't* make the water translucent.

The first layer went in the deeper areas, ending in a very distinct line. The blue was too dark to continue under the bridge into the narrows, and so this distinct edge had to be disguised. We tried to pour a second batch while the first one was still fluid so we could diffuse the edges, but we were too late.

Meanwhile, the second batch was setting, so without much thought we mixed some artist's white oil paint from a tube into the green-dyed polyester (green

In this idyllic scene Kyle Williams' GP38 heads up a freight train out of Regis, heading back down to Chateaugay. The crystal-clear stream is shallow and the bottom is visible because no coloring was added to the polyester. The author likes to use polyester because it ripples naturally.

because we were pouring the sluggish stream). A third batch of clear polyester was poured above the deep blue area, and the clear and murky green mix were swirled together, in the direction of the flow of the stream, to make the transition. After wiping the sweat from our brows, we realized it wasn't half bad, and in fact have received a number of compliments on this.

LESSONS LEARNED

Based on our experiences at the RPI club, I've learned some lessons about modeling water and have drawn the following conclusions:

• Of all the currently available materials, polyester gives the best results. It's transparent, it provides surface texture, and it can be colored.

• Surface texture and coloring are more important than transparency, so that other methods that capture these two can be almost as effective, especially from low-angle viewing.

• When the water is shallow, the bottom can be seen, so it should be modeled with little or no coloring added.

• When modeling deeper water, except along the shoreline, you should not be able to see bottom. This appearance of depth can be accomplished by adding coloring to the polyester.

• Oil paint can be mixed with the polyester in lieu of, or in conjunction with, dyes.

• Finally, because we can't provide enough diffuse blue light inside to give enough reflections, we need to compensate by adding blue pigment to the water.

Maybe those young artists with the blue crayons are right after all! ✿

This high-angle photograph taken at Hastings Bay (compare this with the low-angle photo of the same scene on page 44) illustrates the author's description of how, in the "heat of the pour," club members discovered that artist's oil paint can be mixed with polyester — with good results.

The author used acrylic gloss medium to rejuvenate and add waves to Baker Stream on his Carrabasset & Dead River Ry., brushing the medium over the old, scratched epoxy surface.

Fig. 1. Here's the equipment needed to model gloss medium water. Right is the medium; center are tube acrylic paints for tinting. Brushing on the medium with different-sized brushes results in various wave patterns and effects.

Fig. 2. Right. The first step in modeling a body of water is painting the flat bottom with latex paint. Author Frary uses a flat black for the deep areas, earth color for the shallows. **Next right.** He adds rocks and sand along the banks and fixes them in place with a dilute solution of matte medium.

Modeling water
with acrylic gloss medium

Easy techniques for making
realistically rippled streams, lakes, and waterfront scenery

BY DAVE FRARY

PHOTOS BY THE AUTHOR

OVER the past several years I've experimented a lot with water modeling techniques. One material I've been using is acrylic gloss medium, and the more I use it, the better I like it. Placid pools, rushing rapids, ice and snow — acrylic gloss medium works great for all of them.

Besides its versatility, gloss medium has other advantages over the other two popular water modeling media, polyester resin and two-part epoxy. With gloss medium there's no mixing of two separate parts — like paint, it comes in a single container. There's no offensive odor and little hazard. Gloss medium goes exactly where you put it and doesn't creep up onto river banks as other water media do. It's nontoxic and you can clean up all your tools with water.

Gloss medium is an acrylic varnish and you'll find it in stores that sell art supplies. Among the frequently found brands are Grumbacher, Liquitex, and Utrect Linen. Artists use the medium as a clear, protective coating for paintings

and sometimes mix it with acrylic paints to alter their working properties. Gloss medium has the same characteristics as acrylic matte medium, a material most model railroaders are familiar with as it has been used for years as an adhesive to bond ballast and scenery material in place. The big difference is that matte medium dries flat whereas gloss medium dries to a high gloss.

As it comes from the bottle or can, gloss medium is a thick white goop with a brushing consistency similar to that of latex house paint. You can thin it with water, but doing so diminishes its glossiness, which is, of course, the very property that makes it useful for modeling water in the first place.

Given typical indoor temperature and humidity, gloss medium dries crystal-clear in 20 to 30 minutes; once dry it is water- and oil-resistant. Because it is an acrylic emulsion it is compatible with and can be colored with acrylic paints, Polly S model paints, and other water-soluble colors.

Shown in fig. 1 are the only tools you'll need to build gloss medium water on your layout or diorama. You probably already have brushes in several different sizes and a shallow pan or tray to hold the medium while you add color to it.

THE LOOK OF DEPTH

The model water you see in these photos has no real depth — it's simply a glossy, reflective coating applied to a flat surface. The illusion of depth is created with paint. Before you start shouting that you're no great shakes at painting, be advised it's easy.

Figure 2 shows the basic idea. On this HO oceanfront diorama the flat water surface is Masonite. After building up the scenery along the water's edge I sealed the Masonite with a heavy coat of flat black latex paint. After this dried I painted the areas where sand and rocks would be with Polly S Earth, then sprinkled on the scenery materials.

Using a soft brush I shifted the texture materials around until I liked their position then soaked them with a bonding solution of 1 part acrylic matte medium diluted with 5 parts water and a few drops of liquid dishwashing detergent. This is the standard bonding solution I always use for scenery materials; I prefer it to dilute white glue because it dries perfectly flat.

I let the matte medium bonding solution dry overnight, then vacuumed up any texture material that was still loose. To blend the shallow areas into the deep

Fig. 3. Painting a thinned solution of gloss medium to the high water mark creates the look of low tide. Tires and other details are added.

Fig. 4. Left. The author builds up his gloss medium water in layers, tinting the early coats with acrylics. A black tint creates the illusion of depth in deep water areas. **Above.** A brown tint gives a silty look to shallows. A little blue added to later layers suggested reflected sky.

water, I airbrushed Polly S Earth along the edges, lightly feathering the Earth color into the black. This feathering provides the basic illusion of depth we're after, and until you try it yourself you can't appreciate how effective it is. You can simulate sandbars and other shallow areas by misting thinned Earth color over the black paint.

Airbrushing is by far the easiest and fastest way of feathering the shallow and deep areas together, but if you don't have an airbrush you can apply earth-colored paint with a spray can or a brush. If you use a brush, thin 1 part Polly S Earth with 3 parts water and dab it on using only the tip of the brush. Apply less and less paint as you move out from the shore toward the deep water.

THE LOOK OF LOW TIDE

Once the banks and the water surface are colored, textured, and dry, it's time for the gloss medium. If you want to build a low-tide oceanfront scene, begin by thinning a small amount of gloss medium with an equal amount of water. Brush this mixture over all the rocks, sand, seaweed, and other surfaces up to the high-tide line. Like I said earlier, thinning gloss medium eliminates some of its shine, but that's just the effect you want here. It makes the shoreline look as if the tide is out and those objects once covered with water have only partially dried.

While the shoreline is still wet with the dilute gloss medium, I add a few extra details: driftwood, old tires, barrels, and so forth, as shown in fig. 3. I set each detail in place using a small dab of gloss medium as the adhesive.

LAYER BY LAYER

I build up the gloss medium water in layers, coloring each layer with tube acrylics to further create illusions of depth or turbulence. By using different-size brushes you can manipulate the water surface to represent everything from slightly rippled ponds to fast-moving rapids and waterfalls.

For the first layer on my oceanfront scene I added ¼" of Mars Black acrylic tube color to ½ cup of gloss medium. That ¼" is the amount of paint squeezed from the tube, give or take a millihair. Obviously, it's far from a scientific measurement, but for a project like this it's plenty good enough. When in doubt remember that in scenery building it's usually better to have too little color than too much.

I brushed the black-tinted gloss medium onto the deep water areas to add the illusion of even greater depth, as shown in fig. 4. I wasn't trying to texture the gloss medium with this first coat, just brushing it on as smoothly as I could.

For the next layer of gloss medium I added ⅛" each (just a dab, really) of Raw Sienna and Burnt Umber tube acrylics to a half cup of medium. After mixing this thoroughly I brushed it over the sand, rocks, and shallow water areas from the shoreline out into the deep water, trying my best to blend this brown-tinted gloss medium into the areas previously treated with the black-tinted. There should be no sharp lines between the shallow and deep areas. This brown layer adds the look of sand and silt to the shallows.

Fig. 6. Laying on the medium in long strokes with a palette knife will create the look of gentle swells. This should be easy for anyone who's frosted a cake!

Fig. 7. Our author has found gloss medium quite good for modeling snow and ice. His snow is acrylic paste coated with clear medium.

Fig. 5. Left. Stippling the final clear coats creates the look of rippling water. Above. The gloss medium dries crystal clear. The wave patterns can be subtle yet quite effective.

ADDING RIPPLES AND WAVES

After the initial applications of tinted gloss medium have dried, it's time to evaluate the results. Often you'll find the colors just right and can go ahead with untinted gloss medium to texture and build up the surface. On the ocean-front diorama I decided to add some layers of blue-tinted medium to slightly color the water and make the transitions between the shallow and deep areas more subtle. I mixed ¼" of Ultra Blue tube color with one cup of gloss medium and applied this over the entire water surface, swirling it on quickly and allow ing it to dry, undisturbed, for approximately 10 minutes.

The 10-minute wait gave the gloss medium time to stiffen slightly, and I then textured the surface with a small, stiff brush to make it look like wind-blown water. Repeatedly dabbing the brush into the thickened gloss medium left small, random piles of the material.

As the gloss medium dried it shrank slightly, and the texture became gentler and more subtle. Once the first coat had dried thoroughly I applied two more blue-tinted coats, allowing each to dry before adding the next. I found the hint of blue added a transparent haze effect that gave the water a touch of mystery and extra depth.

For the final coat I brushed on clear, untinted gloss medium as shown in fig. 5. Then I took a small brush and added extra plain gloss medium around the bases of the pilings to represent swirls and ripples.

The gloss medium makes such good waves and ripples that it's possible to have unrealistically high seas. To cure this problem, should it occur, use a block covered with fine sandpaper to sand the crests off the waves. Mop up all the sanding dust with a damp cloth and apply a smooth coat of plain gloss medium, brushing it out well in the troughs between the wave tops.

WHITE WATER AND BROWN WATER

I have experimented with gloss medium to represent different types of wa-

ter surfaces, and in my opinion it's by far the easiest to use for the white water in swift-flowing mountain streams, waterfalls, rapids, and ocean whitecaps.

To add white water effects mix a very small amount of Titanium White tube acrylic with a tablespoon of gloss medium. Use a small brush to stipple this white mixture onto wave tops, around obstacles in the water, and anywhere else that white water would occur. A few color photos from a magazine like National Geographic are handy for getting the locations of the white water right. You won't be able to judge your results right away, so wait until the first application dries before adding more white. Bear in mind that a little white goes a long way.

As shown in fig. 6, you can simulate slow-moving, muddy water by adding a tad of Polly S Mud to the gloss medium. Apply it to the flat base with a palette knife (a butter knife will also do in a pinch). The knife allows you to lay the gloss medium on with broader strokes than are possible with a brush. Muddy water is pretty much opaque, so if you

color each of the gloss medium layers, very little painting of the flat base itself will be required.

MODELING FROZEN WATER

Gloss medium is also great for making snow and icicles for winter scenes. See fig. 7. I model snow on buildings by brushing acrylic modeling paste onto horizontal surfaces, then coating it with gloss medium after it dries. This modeling paste is a pure-white medium intended for building up heavy texture on acrylic paintings.

To make icicles glue short lengths of clear fishing leader or toothbrush bristles in place with dabs of gloss medium, then coat them with more gloss medium to build up the icicle shape.

Try gloss medium water on a small section of your railroad or on a diorama, and see if you don't agree with me that this material is easy to use and gives realistic results. As a bonus, if acrylic gloss medium water gets scratched or dirty, you need only apply another thin coat of gloss medium to make it look like new again, maybe even better! ⚙

The water seen here appears to have great depth, but it's simply built up with thin layers of gloss medium. The medium can be tinted with tube acrylic paints to create all sorts of special effects.

A household sponge worked beautifully for adding waves to this water created with joint compound.

Sponge modeling

Modeling water and roads with joint compound

BY JIM KELLY
PHOTOS BY THE AUTHOR

OKAY, so what we're really talking about here is modeling with joint compound. "Sponge modeling" makes a snappier title, though, and a common household sponge is the most useful tool I've found for working with this extremely versatile material.

Joint compound is that plaster-like material used to seal over joints in drywall construction. You can buy it in any hardware or building supply store. It comes premixed in a ½-gallon bucket (enough to last a lifetime doing the sorts of projects I'll describe here) and costs about four bucks.

Two characteristics of joint compound make it an extremely useful modeling material. First, it sets very slowly, so you have as much time as you want to work and shape the surface. Second, once it's dry, it's water soluble. You can wipe it to a smooth finish with a wet sponge. This was pointed out to me by a friend, Dick Cecil, only after I'd spent hours sanding joints on my layout's backdrop, getting joint compound dust

Fig. 1 SPONGE WATER

Smooth on joint compound

Dab on waves with sponge

Paint su

Fig. 2 SPONGE ROAD

Model road with Sculptamold

Add thin layer of joint compound

all over the basement and spitting it for two days after.

SPONGE WATER

Figure 1 shows how I used joint compound to model water. I spread a thin layer (about 1/16" to 1/8" deep on the plywood base, smoothing it on as evenly as I could with a putty knife).

I created the waves by dabbing at the surface with a common household synthetic sponge, the kind you can buy at the grocery store, usually in a package of three for about a dollar.

With a little practice you'll find all sorts of wave patterns can be created. For choppy water just dab randomly with the flat side of the sponge. For parallel lines of waves make a series of dabs with the edge, holding the sponge the same way for each move, sort of as if you're chopping off sections of carrot with a sharp knife. By pulling a little to one side as you lift the sponge you can make neat little curling caps on the waves.

I had two small problems. One was cracks here and there — joint compound shrinks as it dries and tends to crack if there's much thickness to it at all. I fixed this by brushing more compound into the cracks, using a flat paintbrush. This cure had the added advantage of introducing a little more interesting texture to the surface.

The other problem was keeping the waves small enough for an N scale lake. The solution was just to work carefully and let the material stiffen some before working it with the sponge.

When the compound had thoroughly dried, I airbrushed Floquil's Earth along the banks, then airbrushed the water surface with Dark Blue. The idea here is to carry the earth color out into the water surface a short distance and feather it into the blue color. The result will suggest shallow water near the banks.

I finished the water by brushing on a heavy coat of gloss medium, then adding a second after the first dried. This is a clear acrylic varnish you can buy at art supply stores. Dave Frary explored its uses fully in the January 1984 MR.

Just like the water on page 52, the road here was created with a joint compound. For twisting, turning roads, there's no technique better.

A SPONGE ROAD

The road I made with joint compound is shown in fig. 2. First I modeled the road as smooth as I could using Sculptamold, a plaster-like modeling material available at art stores. You could also use plaster.

Once this subroad was dry, I topped it with a thin layer of joint compound and waited for several days until it dried. Then I smoothed the surface by gently wiping it with a wet sponge. If you try this you'll find that not much happens at first; then the surface begins to come smooth and the tool marks and irregularities begin disappearing. You should keep a bucket of water handy and rinse out your sponge occasionally.

I finished the road by airbrushing it with Floquil's Southern Pacific gray and adding lines, using Floquil paint in a ruling pen.

The results are very pleasing to me because I've never quite been happy with roads I've made before. I could never get plaster or Sculptamold smooth enough to suit me. I've made good-looking roads with sheet styrene, although these tend to come out artificially flat — a road should be slightly crowned in the middle and fall off to each side for proper drainage. For twisting, turning roads, I think this sponge technique would be hard to beat.

I find it fascinating that the same material worked well for two such entirely different projects, and I imagine some of you scenery pros will find even more uses for this extremely versatile product. ◊

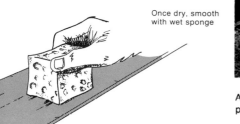

Brush on gloss medium

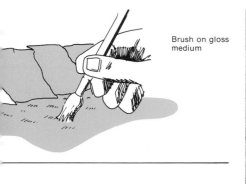

Once dry, smooth with wet sponge

A wet sponge works well for smoothing the dry surface of a joint compound road. Nothing will happen immediately after you apply the sponge, but eventually the surface will begin to smooth.

White water on the Denver & Rio Chama Western

A step-by-step description of how to model rapids, rushing streams, and waterfalls

BY MALCOLM FURLOW

THE 3-foot gauge engines and cars of the Colorado mountain-carriers (the powerful Denver & Rio Grande, the Rio Grande Southern, and other Otto Mears' roads) were fed into the awesome passes and ravines of the towering Uncompahgre Mountains. Clinging precariously to sheer rock cliffs, the rails made their way along such white-water streams as the Animas, Clear Creek, and the Gunnison.

The slim gauge steam cars twisted along these streams and rivers, carrying the hardrock miners, the drummers for whiskey firms, the Irish bartenders, the gamblers, and the madames — all on their way to the false-front buildings and wooden-plank walkways of hastily built little mining towns.

These marks of man fade quickly in the Colorado high places. The intense winters and the rivers that swell to overflowing during the spring thaw are quick to reclaim the grades of vanished railroads.

But the rivers remain.

These white-water streams and rivers are extremely beautiful and offer a challenge to those of us who would try to recreate a little of the beauty of Narrow Gauge Country. At the beginning of last summer, I packed my camera in my suitcase and, with the family snuggly stuffed into our rather smallish Pontiac, drove to the region of the shining mountains to record for myself the majesty of Colorado's whitewater streams and rivers.

With this accomplished we drove home to Dallas to rest our hiked-out bodies and to start going over the slides for ideas about a white-water stream or two for the Rio Chama. The ideas presented here are not new, but a few things I've learned through experimentation may make the going a bit easier for those who enjoy this facet of scenery construction. Since creating white water — waterfalls, rapids, whirlpools, and rushing streams — may very well be the most difficult type of water to model on a layout, I suggest you read carefully and follow the photographs. They should help you visualize the steps described.

FORMING THE RIVERBED BASE

The base for the riverbed is paper (grocery bag paper or industrial hand towels) dipped in Hydrocal, a very hard plaster used as a base for other scenery materials and formed over a depression in the bench-

The first step was to create a depression in the benchwork. The Homasote base is about 1" down.

Be sure to seal all seams when pouring in the plaster subbase. Resin will find all holes you leave.

Once you have placed all detail you want in the riverbed, soak it well with diluted white glue.

work. Make sure the plaster is sealed around all seams, because the casting resin used to create the water effect will find even the smallest pinhole to escape through. If the river is placed so as to flow off the table edge, you will need to construct some sort of dam to keep the resin from decorating the floor. Cardboard taped to the edge will work. Be sure to lay rags or paper underneath the layout (just in case). You can remove the makeshift dam when the resin has dried.

DETAILING THE RIVERBED

The riverbed itself is a mixture of various sizes of rocks and gravel, with simulated rotted timbers, small twigs, old tires, and anything else you might use to enhance the scene. Got a car or vehicle that didn't turn out right? Throw it in the river!

If any waterfalls are to be included, I suggest you make them from angel hair. The easiest place to find angel hair is in a pet shop. It's the material used for aquarium filters. There seem to be two types: one is soft, rather kinky, and without sheen (this is *not* the kind you want); the other resembles Fiberglas. It's shiny and comes in straight strands (*this* is the kind you want). A word of caution about working with it: it's like working with Fiberglas insulation. Little bits and pieces can work their way into your skin and irritate it, so handle it carefully.

Only a small amount is necessary. Comb the angel hair and trim it to length, then use ACC to glue it in place at the waterfall site. The angel hair will serve to direct the flow of the casting resin.

Before adding resin, everything in the riverbed should be secured in place with a mixture of white glue and water. Thin the

glue to a 1:1 mixture and add a few drops of liquid detergent. The liquid detergent acts as a wetting agent. If you use real dirt and rocks for the formation of the banks, be sure you seal this with a good soaking of this glue mixture. The dirt has a tendency to soak up casting resin. Also, be sure not to leave any loose dirt or rock particles, because this will keep the resin from adhering to the river bottom and sometimes creates unnatural-looking bubbles on the surface of the casting resin. It's a good idea to wash any natural rocks or scenery materials to remove loose dust.

Also, the casting resin has a tendency to creep up the sides of the banks a little, so after the resin has dried, it would be a good idea to go back and retouch the banks with more dirt and rocks. If you plan to include any weeds along the river edge this is a good time to place them.

The next step, if you're building a waterfall, is to place the angel hair and apply resin thinly.

Blowing air against the flowing resin helps to form ripples on the surface and speeds drying.

During the gelling state, rapids can be formed by picking at the surface with a pointed object.

The high points of the roughed-up area can now be dry-brushed with some acrylic white paint.

Before you apply the resin, be sure the riverbed scene pleases you. Maybe a rock needs to be moved or taken away, or perhaps more rotted timber or twigs along the bank are called for. Make sure that any of the plaster foundation that happens to be peeking through the riverbed is either colored to match the scenery or covered up completely by dirt or gravel. These things must be done before any casting resin is added — it's too late to make any changes afterwards.

Before going on to the next step, let's talk a bit more about the casting resin itself. Using casting resin can be somewhat irritating to the ol' nostrils, so be sure that you provide for adequate ventilation. Also, the containers used in mixing the resin must be of the throwaway variety, because once the plastic hardens it's there for good. Paper cups work fine, but some plastic cups will soften from the action of the resin.

Getting the hang of working with this material is a bit tricky at first. Experimentation on a small diorama would help. But all new materials and methods take some practice.

MIXING THE RESIN

Mix the casting resin according to the manufacturer's recommendations, but add a few more drops of hardener than is actually called for. This will cause more heat during the gelling stage, creating the ripple effect. Any color tinting of the resin is done during the mixing procedure. Various dyes of green, blue, and brown can be purchased at a craft store. These dyes are especially made to be used with the casting resin, and only a very small amount is needed to color the resin. You will also need to purchase some pearl tints for rapids.

Once the first batch of resin has been mixed, add a little blue-green dye and pour in the first coating of resin, not more than ¼" deep. It can be poured a little thicker, but try not to go over ½" or cracking could occur during the hardening stage. The thicker the layer, the more heat it produces. If you wish to give the illusion of more depth, stir in a bit more blue-green dye rather than trying to pour several layers of resin.

While the casting resin is setting, you can use a hair dryer to speed up the action. Be careful not to get so close as to actually burn the plastic. Use of the hair dryer will also keep a lot of the resin from flowing over the waterfall (to be formed from pearl-tinted resin) and will create more ripples.

Mix another batch of resin using *only* a very small amount of pearl tint (one-half drop per ounce) and pour it over the falls. Start at the top and use the hair dryer to keep the flow back. Experiment with the angle of the hair dryer, trying to keep most of the resin on the angel hair. The resin flows down like water (though not as fast), but the force of the air from the hair dryer will help keep the resin on the angel hair.

Before the resin has completely set, take an ice pick or some hard, pointed object and manipulate the resin into ripples and waves. The gel state lasts for only a few minutes, so work quickly. After the waterfall has set, dry-brush the falls using a stiff-bristled paintbrush and small amounts of acrylic white paint.

Now, move on to the next coating of resin. Mix another batch, using a little less of the blue-green dye, and pour it into the river area. Repeat the procedure with the hair dryer. A note on coloring: It is better to mix in too little color than too much. Exercise a light hand. When this batch of resin has reached the gelling stage, begin creating rapids by picking the resin with a pointed instrument — forming peaks and valleys. Rapids should be formed around areas of rocks, timbers, and shallow areas.

When this batch has set and the last picks of the resin have been made, begin dabbing in this area with the stiff brush dipped in a minute amount of white paint. Touch only the high points. Only the rapids and waterfalls are to be given this treatment; you want the rest of the river to remain blue-green.

Mix a final batch of casting resin, omitting any dyes or colors. This batch should be applied with a disposable brush over the entire stream, including the waterfalls, to achieve a wet look.

Creating white water may very well be the most difficult type of water to model on a layout. On the other hand, it may very well be the most effective scenery on your layout. I think it's worth the effort. ⚙

Work on the lower falls was started at a later time because of the small amounts of resin being used. It seems that smaller waterfalls are a bit more realistic when subjected to viewing from close up.

A trimmed, reworked, and painted pole takes on a realistic, weathered appearance. The insulators are painted green and coated with clear gloss to represent glass.

Improved line poles

A simple method of modifying commercial plastic line poles

BY LOU SASSI

PROMINENT FEATURES along railroad rights-of-way are the line poles that are used for communication and signaling. The HO scale telephone poles in the Atlas no. 775 pack (12 per pack) are well proportioned and available at a reasonable price; their appearance, however, can be improved. With paint, a few tools, and a little work, I've found I can make them much more presentable for use on my HO scale Postabe RR.

First, notch the pole at the bottom and snap off the cast-on base. I prefer only one or two cross arms, so I cut off one or two of the top cross arms and then bevel the top of the pole with a file.

With a sharp razor-saw blade, scrape wood grain striations lengthwise into the pole and the cross arms; then brush with Floquil Reefer Gray. Work rapidly or the paint will attack the plastic. When the paint has set, apply ground dry pigment colors with a dry brush. Work these colors in until you achieve a streaked brown and black coloring. I use Windsor & Newton black and raw umber dry pigments. These are available at many art supply stores. Empire White and Color-Rite dry pigments are available from some model suppliers such as Wm. K. Walthers.

Paint the insulators Floquil Dark Green. When dry, coat them with Floquil Clear High Gloss so they will look like glass. The angle braces supporting the cross arms are to be painted Grimy Black.

I install the poles by drilling 1/8"-diameter holes in the track base a scale 14 feet out from the rail center line, spacing them about 100 feet (13.75") apart. The reworked poles add a great deal to the visual appearance of the model right-of-way. Fine thread or wire can be attached to the insulators to represent the wires, although I did not do this. For more information on line poles see the October 1981 MODEL RAILROADER Closeup article titled "Railroad line poles." ❖

The out-of-the-box line pole lacks realism; the drawing shows the author's changes.

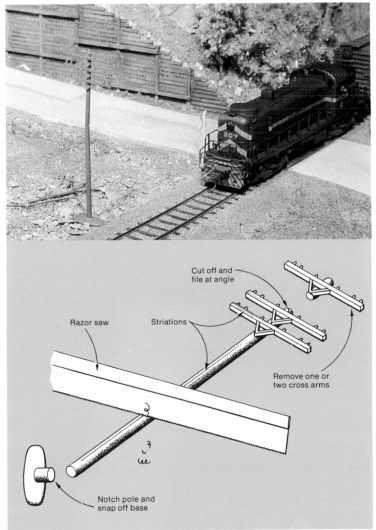

Cut off and file at angle

Razor saw

Striations

Remove one or two cross arms

Notch pole and snap off base

Making signs for the layout

An expert modeler
shares a wealth
of proven techniques

Our author adds an iceberg to a sign made with dry transfers. Brushwork is tricky, requires some artistic skill, but is seldom required to make signs. Here it adds a distinctive touch.

BY EARL SMALLSHAW
PHOTOS BY THE AUTHOR

SIGNS are among the most important details you can add to a model railroad. Just look at what signs contribute:

• Signs bring life to the scene, implying that people are coming and going. Who would bother to put up signs where there were no people to read them?

• Signs help establish the era modeled. A billboard selling a 1922 Ford wouldn't be found on a contemporary railroad, for example.

• Signs identify geography. An "Ohio Paper Co." sign implies that the layout is in Ohio, or at least in the general area of Ohio.

• Signs give structures purpose and identity. Boxcars delivered to a large, signless structure do little for our imaginations as compared to the same structure identifed as the "Middletown Container Co.," and listing "Boxes, crates, and kegs" as its products.

• And signs add interest and character to the scene. How blah the city would look without signs on the walls, rooftops, and streets.

DRY TRANSFER SIGNS

For making your own signs dry transfers are the easiest material to use. You can mix and match type styles and sizes to achieve almost any result. Manufacturers such as C-THRU, Letraset, and Press Type offer countless letter styles and sizes; these are found at most art supply stores.

Before we get into dry-transfer lettering techniques, I'd like to mention a tool made expressly for dry-transfer application. It has a handle about the size of an X-acto knife, with three interchangeable tips, as shown in fig 1. Now, I know you can rub on dry-transfer letters with a pencil or ballpoint pen, but this tool, available for about $2 to $3 at an art supply store, does a much better job. I wouldn't use anything else.

If your sign will have a background color, paint it first. I prefer to use an

airbrush for even paint distribution, but brush painting is also acceptable.

Once I have determined the wording for a sign, I place a sheet of tracing paper over the dry-transfer alphabet set and trace the letters one by one. This step ensures that the wording will fit in the space selected, and it also provides a guide for spacing the letters when I apply them.

I tape this piece of tracing paper on the structure, centering the wording just below where the dry transfers will go, then apply the letters, checking their locations against the traced lettering as I go. To make sure the lettering bonds well, I burnish it by placing blank areas of the transfer sheet over the applied letters and rubbing with my transfer application tool.

Several techniques make it possible to use dry transfers for lettering in any color. For my "Poli Ice Co." lettering I used a C-THRU Helvetica Outline Medium alphabet. This set provides only black outlines, allowing the background color to show. If another color is desired, simply paint that color between the lines, as shown in fig. 2. I use Floquil's no. 0 brush. As you learned from your childhood coloring books, don't go outside the lines!

Another way to color lettering is the lift-off technique, illustrated in fig. 3. First paint the sign the color you want the letters to be. Once the paint is dry apply the dry transfer letters, but don't burnish them as in a normal application.

Next, airbrush the background color over the entire sign. After the paint is dry, use a strip of Scotch tape to carefully peel the dry transfer letters away, exposing the original panel color.

MAKING STENCILED SIGNS

Figure 4 shows a Coca-Cola sign I made with a stencil. Coca-Cola spells out its name in the very same script it used 80 years ago, but the price has changed

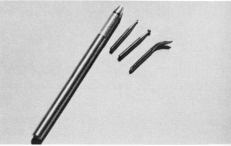

Fig. 1. Top. Dry transfers come in a wide variety of type styles and sizes. **Middle.** Although transfers can be rubbed on with a pencil, our author recommends using a specially made burnishing tool. **Above.** Our author traces the letters off the alphabet sheet onto tracing paper, then tapes the paper in position to use as a lettering guide.

Fig. 2. One technique for colorful signs is painting the insides of outline letters with a brush.

Fig. 3. With the lift-off technique, letters of any color can appear on a background of any color. Paint the lettering color, add the transfers, paint the background, then pick away the transfers.

and so has the slogan. One of the modern slogans such as "Coke is it" or "Things go better with Coke" would have destroyed the validity of the period ad that I intended to create.

I tried in vain to find the Coca-Cola slogan used around 1920 and was about to write to the company when a friend showed me a book on collectibles. In it Coca-Cola trays were illustrated, along with the year they were brought out.

The trays also carried a slogan. To make this story short, "Delicious and refreshing" was Coke's slogan around 1922. But, back to the stenciling.

I spotted a photo in my local newspaper showing a Coca-Cola sign hanging from a storefront. It was exactly the size I required. With rubber cement (white glue would also do), I glued the newspaper sign to an IBM card. Once dry, I carefully cut out the words "Coca-Cola,"

using an X-acto knife with a new no. 11 blade. This is no place to cheap-out with that dull blade you've been using for the last 2 months. For an intricate stencil such as this, the blade must be absolutely sharp!

In tracing the words, I made sure to leave thin bridges connecting the outsides and centers of the O's, L's, and A's.

Once I was through cutting I turned the sign over and made sure the cut lines met. Then I gently — *very* gently — removed the letters. A toothpick and my X-acto knife worked well in lifting the delicate letters from the stencil.

Since Coca-Cola signs usually have white letters on a bright red background, I masked off an area on my building and airbrushed it with Floquil Caboose Red. After the paint dried, I centered the stencil on this red panel and affixed it with drafting tape, making sure it lay flat.

The "5¢" called for another stencil, one that was obviously much easier to make. With both stencils positioned, I masked off the remainder of the red panel and the structure.

Next I sprayed on Floquil Reefer White, holding the airbrush so it was perpendicular to the surface. If the airbrush is held at an angle, paint can get under the stencil, causing overspray.

If painted properly, all the letters will have sharp definition. Some touchup work is required, however. Those bridges that held the centers of the letters must be painted out by hand. I used a Floquil no. 0 brush. Any small errors or a little overspray can be corrected by touching up with the red.

To complete the lettering on the sign, I used three different dry-transfer alphabet sets. For the border I cut very thin (¹/₃₂″) strips from white decal paper. To allow for positioning, I made the strips

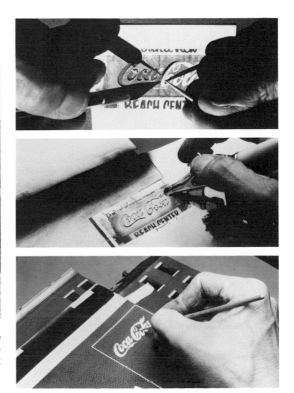

Fig. 4. Above. Our author used a stencil to re-create Coca-Cola's distinctive trademark. He began by cementing a newspaper illustration to a file card. Upper right. He cut around the lettering, then used the tip of an X-acto blade and a toothpick to extract the cut-out pieces. Middle right. Using an airbrush he painted the lettering onto the building's side. Lower right. A brush was used to paint out the tiny bridges holding the centers of letters.

Fig. 5. Top. Small signs can be made from copy machine reductions. Above. Our author colored the letters with a yellow highlighter, then darkened the black area with a felt-tip pen. Right. Colored pencils were used to give the lettering a more golden look.

somewhat longer than needed, and then I used an X-acto knife to trim the corners where the strips overlapped. Solvaset nestled the decal down onto the brickwork. (Dry-transfer lines can also be used for borders.)

I dry-brushed on some powered white chalk to fade my sign. Black chalk dust added the grime that has accumulated over the years.

PHOTOCOPY SIGNS

Sometimes the sign you want is just too small to make with available dry-transfer letter sets. This is particularly true for those modelers who work in the smaller scales.

In today's offices there's almost always a photocopy machine that's capable of making enlarged or reduced copies. For our purposes, the reduction feature is most useful.

Figure 5 shows a sign I made using a copying machine. With dry-transfer letters I first composed a sign on a piece of paper in the normal manner. Using the photocopier, I reduced the sign to 66 percent of the original size, the maximum my copier would allow. The resulting sign was still too large, so I copied the copy, reducing to 66 percent again. This process was repeated until I achieved the size I desired. Not only was the sign reduced, but any imperfections in the original lettering were minimized with each reduction.

If you want colored letters you can used felt-tip pens. I used a High Liter (yellow) to color "Bascom's Boots." Some touchup of the black background may be

necessary, using a fine-point, black felt-tip pen.

I used rubber cement to glue the paper sign to an index card. The yellow lettering was a little bright for my purposes, as I was attempting to achieve the "gold" lettering found on many stores back in the 1920s. With colored pencils of orange and brown, I was able to modify the bright yellow into the aged, gold color I wanted.

SOURCES FOR SIGNS

So much for making your own signs. You can also use signs that someone else has made for you. Those modeling the contemporary scene can find sign material everywhere — in magazines and Sunday newspaper supplements, on product containers, etc.

The period modeler has to be more resourceful. Occasionally, a modern ad will feature advertisements from the past. A few years ago Camel cigarettes ran three different ads, all reproductions of ads 50 to 60 years prior.

Now and then MODEL RAILROADER reproduces signs from the steam era. In past issues there have been recruiting posters, circus posters, automobile billboards, and more.

Commercial signs are offered by Vintage Reproductions, Fine Scale Miniatures, Woodland Scenics, and others. Vintage and Woodland Scenics provide their signs in dry-transfer form.

Although signs, in most cases, have no scale (a small sign in O scale is a big sign in HO or N), your selection of sign material should be in keeping with the

scale you are modeling. Obviously, if you want small signs, then use the advertisements from small magazines such as *Reader's Digest*. The Sunday newspaper supplements, particularly the coupon ads, are another good source of small advertisements.

Sign material is everywhere. The trick is to become sign-conscious. As you come across potential signs in magazines and newspapers, clip them out and store them in an old shoe box. Soon you'll have a nice selection.

SANDING PAPER SIGNS

Most of the paper signs from your shoe box are too thick to be applied directly to the wall of a structure. See fig. 6. Paper signs can be thinned to scale thickness (or close to it) by careful sanding.

You'll need a small roll of drafting tape from your local art supply store. This tape sticks to paper but can be removed easily without damage. Normal masking tape, duct tape, etc., should not be used; it's just too sticky.

First cut a piece of tape about ¼" to ⅜" square and place it in the center of the back of the sign. Cut a larger piece of tape about ⅛" to ¼" smaller all around than your sign and lay it directly over the first. The object is to protect the sign during the sanding process.

Using a very fine sandpaper, sand from the center of the sign outward, using very light strokes, and distributing the sanding equally around the full perimeter of the sign.

Once the edge of the sign has been reduced to the limit without breaking

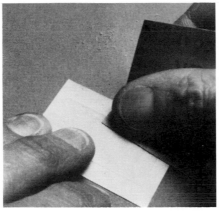

Fig. 6. **Left.** The lower sign has been sanded to scale thickness and settles into the brick joints as a real paper sign would. **Right.** Our author protects the sign's middle with tape while sanding the outside edges. He sands the center last.

applications. The decals produced don't approach the quality of those we use on our rolling stock, but they're adequate for sign purposes.

There is nothing difficult about this process. Simply cut your sign from the magazine, allowing about ¼" extra on all four sides. Then brush the Decal It on the sign's surface, spreading it as evenly as possible, as shown in fig. 7. Allow it to dry.

The Decal It instructions suggest six applications, but that's for the decoupage folks. We want a decal as thin as possible, so I use two applications. At this point, the magazine image has been transformed into a decal, but the paper backing must be removed.

Submerge the decal in a shallow dish of warm water with a couple of drops of liquid detergent added. Eventually the paper will soak off, although you can speed up the process by gently peeling off layers of paper with tweezers. Once you see the backside of the decal appear, you're ready to apply your sign. But first, trim that ¼" from each side to get a clean edge to the decal.

For my decal sign I used an enlistment poster from a July 1976 issue of MODEL RAILROADER. Since the decal had a clear background, I had to paint a white panel on the wall of my structure before the decal was applied, otherwise the brick would have become the background color.

Once the decal was positioned, I used Solvaset to nestle it into the brickwork.

An advantage of the decal is that it gives the appearance of a paper sign without having to do any sanding. Using the decal method for a large sign might be difficult, since the decal is so thin and tends to become distorted with handling. Try a small sign until you become familiar with this process.

These, then, are some of the sign-making techniques you can use to give your layout interest and character. I hope you'll give them a try. ۞

through, remove the top piece of tape.

Again working from the center out, carefully sand the area the first piece of tape covered. Remember, the edges of the sign are already very thin. Further sanding may tear them. If you want an old, weather-beaten sign, sand the edges so they begin to disappear.

Now remove the second piece of tape. A few light sanding strokes in the center and you're finished.

. To apply the sign I first coat the back of it with a mixture of 70 percent white glue and 30 percent water, and then I press it in place. I remove any wrinkles or bubbles by laying a piece of index card over the sign and applying a stroking pressure.

If the sign is to represent one recently posted, then no further work is required. For an older sign you can fashion rips and tears with a modeler's knife while the sign is still moist from being applied. Once the sign is dry, it can be dulled by dry-brushing with black or brown chalk dust.

DECAL SIGNS

There's a product found in art stores called Decal It which will make a decal of almost any picture in a magazine. A small bottle sells for $2 to $3 and will last for a great many decals.

This product is primarily for decoupage hobbyists. It provides them with a thinner-than-paper picture for decoupage

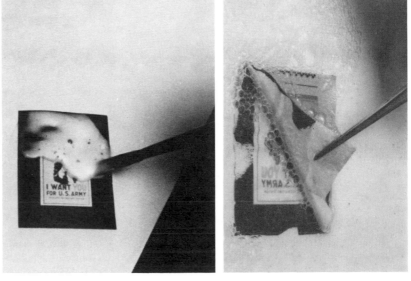

Fig. 7. **Left.** This faded sign is a homemade decal, made with a decoupage product. The starting point was a miniature poster from MODEL RAILROADER. **Middle.** The poster was painted with two applications of Decal It. **Right.** The paper was soaked away, leaving a thin decal.

Summit scenery on the NEB&W

Copying a prototype scene from ground to sky

BY JOHN NEHRICH

PHOTOS BY THE AUTHOR

AN RS-1 fan trip from Steamtown at Bellows Falls, Vt., to Rutland, in the late spring of 1981 gave me firsthand experience of the climb over the Green Mountains. This route is older than any historical record, beginning as an Indian trail, serving as a main line for the former Rutland RR, and winding up as a 50-mile short line called the Green Mountain RR. Listening to the old Alco struggling up the steep inclines, my abstract knowledge of the line came alive.

The ex-Rutland grade swings away from the Connecticut River Valley to follow glaciated, U-shaped valleys up into the mountains. Near Summit a long cut brings it out onto a flat stretch of poorly drained land covered with scrub brush and scraggly pines. Then the railroad finds the Mill River to follow as it plunges down toward Rutland and the Champlain Valley. The story of up-and-over is clear in the change of scenery along the way, as the open terrain at the top contrasts with the steep-walled, flat-bottomed valleys on each side.

The Rensselaer Model Railroad Society's HO scale New England, Berkshire & Western RR [see the November 1983 MODEL RAILROADER] combines features of both the Rutland and the Delaware & Hudson. It includes the Rutland's climb over the Green Mountains, portrayed in representative scenes, and that fan trip showed that we should model the distinctive summit terrain to mark the transition from one watershed to another. The modeled scene occupies a space only 3 feet long by 2 feet wide, but this is sufficient to capture the spirit of the place.

SPECIFIC SCENE COPYING

I shot photos through an open coach window on the fan trip, and one that seemed to best capture the summit scenery became the main reference for the model. Notice that instead of trying to invent "typical" scenery, I copied a specific but representative view. This is like a landscape painter finding a pleasing subject and bringing back notes, sketches, and photographs to follow in a studio.

Copying a specific prototype in this fashion is not the ONLY way to model, but it is an easy way to get realistic results, and it avoids the trap of modeling what you've seen on someone else's layout rather than the real world. I've also found that copying a specific scene leads me to learn new techniques, as a given prototype often requires more than I already know how to do. With a clear goal, if I flounder around I at least know where I'm headed and can see how much farther there is to go.

There's also an advantage in not having to understand the geology. It doesn't matter whether the swampy summit terrain is a result of glaciers that lopped off mountain peaks, or if the Green Mountains are not actually mountains but heavily eroded plateaus. Just as landscape painting was possible before modern geology, you can model scenery by re-creating what you see, whether you know how it got that way or not.

We don't copy out of slavish devotion to the prototype. In this case, we felt free to model the Rutland's Summit, Vt., station and some of the scenery around it just to the right of this unidentified summit scene. You can exercise considerable artistic license, as long as you watch out for the point where there are so many changes that it's better to find a more suitable prototype.

For more complex scenes we have taken dozens of photographs from every possible angle, but one photo was sufficient for this scene. A scene itself suggests how much research is needed, but even if it isn't practical to make field trips, one photo is better than none and can still yield good results. We enjoy the research, and turn out piles of photos that sit next to scenery in progress, but don't let this scare you off if you're tempted to try this method.

Copying a specific scene does take more than just familiarity with the prototype. Memory is not dependable in this regard, as our minds are constantly reorganizing the data. Photographs, especially prints, don't play as many tricks.

I used to build structures directly from

Scenery near Summit, Vt., on the New England, Berkshire & Western represents the actual terrain found at the top of the old Rutland RR's climb over the Green Mountains. Author John Nehrich explains how he and the Rensselaer Model Railroad Society re-created the characteristic prototype scene in HO scale.

slides, using a viewer. Even so, I always found discrepancies between my finished model and the real building, things that would have been easy to correct had I noticed them earlier. I think what happened was reverse hallucination, NOT seeing something that IS there. Converting the slides into prints eliminates the fallibility of memory, because I can look at the prints even as I'm working.

The technique of copying a scene involves choosing a specific place, taking pictures for prints or finding postcards, and referring to the pictures as you work. To me, the idea of following the prototype is really more important than the techniques I used to do it.

BASIC CONSTRUCTION

On the NEB&W, L-girder benchwork supports the track structure shown in fig. 1. Earlier, in building the layout, we tried to economize by using particleboard instead of ¾" plywood for subroadbed, but by the time we got to Summit we knew better. The roadbed itself simulates the profile that real railroads use for good drainage. Besides raising the track several feet above "ground" level, the Homasote is also a good material for holding spikes.

The figure also shows how we superelevate or bank curves with ties glued lengthwise along the line of each outer rail. We feather them down at each end of the curve by sanding and then glue the normal crossties (by Scalecraft) on top. After we gave the ties a light sanding and restained them, Dick Hosmer hand spiked the Precision Scale Products Code 83 and 70 rails.

Following Dick closely, Tony Steele formed the roadbed and ballast shoulders by extruding wet wood putty with several passes of a Plexiglas template, guiding it by sliding it on the rails. This idea came from MODEL RAILROADER's Ma & Pa project railroad series back in 1964 and 1965 [reprinted in the Kalmbach book POPULAR MODEL RAILROADS YOU CAN BUILD].

At first we built just the track, until we knew what we wanted to do with the scene. Later we filled the areas on each side of the track with plywood too.

The backdrop is a vital part of our layout because it separates the many scenes and makes the railroad appear linear: a line going from place to place. The desolate Summit scene simply would not work if you could see the city of Berkshire just beyond. Figure 2 shows how we build backdrops.

We paint backdrops with a primer coat and several color coats of flat sky blue latex. We have no standard sky blue, and each of our backdrop runs varies slightly in both hue and shade. Since it's hard to determine the effect of a whole wall of color from just a small paint chip, I'd advise taking a postcard that shows the sky color you want when you go to the paint store and perhaps even picking a color slightly lighter.

We crumple wire screen, stretch it out, and staple it to the plywood to form gentle rolling undulations and a base for the plaster hardshell layer. At this point it would have been easy to carry the Summit scene to completion, but instead I added screen and hardshell for many feet on each side of Summit, both to be sure that adjacent scenes all mesh, and so that I wouldn't have to fling plaster too near any finished scenery. Then I re-

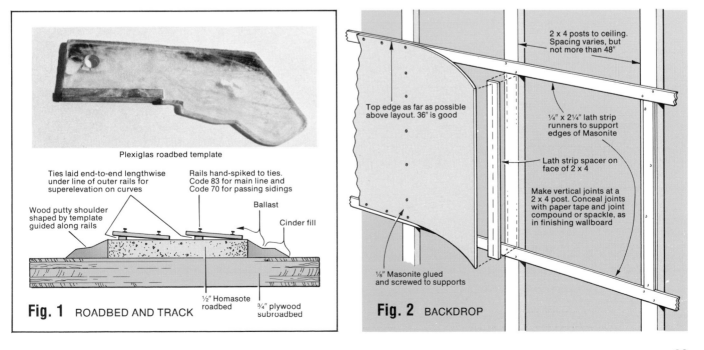

Plexiglas roadbed template

Ties laid end-to-end lengthwise under line of outer rails for superelevation on curves

Rails hand-spiked to ties. Code 83 for main line and Code 70 for passing sidings

Wood putty shoulder shaped by template guided along rails

Ballast

Cinder fill

½" Homasote roadbed

¾" plywood subroadbed

Fig. 1 ROADBED AND TRACK

2 x 4 posts to ceiling. Spacing varies, but not more than 48"

Top edge as far as possible above layout. 36" is good

¼" x 2¼" lath strip runners to support edges of Masonite

Lath strip spacer on face of 2 x 4

Make vertical joints at a 2 x 4 post. Conceal joints with paper tape and joint compound or spackle, as in finishing wallboard

⅛" Masonite glued and screwed to supports

Fig. 2 BACKDROP

Fig. 3. Background flats. Two Masonite cutouts form the background for the summit scene. To texture them, John sprinkled on ground foam, wet the foam with a spray of rubbing alcohol, and bonded it with dilute white glue. The cutouts add a depth and a texture that a painted horizon just wouldn't have.

turned and gave the hardshell a base coat of rich brown latex paint — almost any dark brown or gray will do.

Jeff English ballasted the track, using Highball N scale cinder fill on the lower roadbed shoulders, Highball dark gray HO ballast for the passing siding, and Highball light gray HO ballast on the main. For the look of a well maintained line in the immediate post-war period, he kept the border between ballast and cinders as straight and neat as possible. After shaping the ballast and cinders, Jeff used a window sprayer to wet the ballast with rubbing alcohol and an eyedropper to bond it with diluted white glue. The alcohol wets quicker and better than any combination of water and wetting agent without beading up and disturbing the ballast grains.

MOUNTAIN FLATS

Ed Sproles, a former club member, thought of using foam-covered Masonite cutouts to simulate faraway hills rather than painting these on the backdrop. Just as an artist wouldn't mix oils and pastels on the same canvas, by using ground foam on *both* foreground and background there isn't a distinct change of material, and blending the two takes less work. The texture of the ground foam adds tiny shadows in the coloring, matching the speckled look of the prototype. It's also easier to adjust the cutout to its best location than to adjust a painted line of hills on the backdrop itself.

I cut a rolling profile on a piece of Masonite, put it in position, studied it critically for awhile (I like to go away for a

bit and come back later to see it anew), and then reshaped it until I was satisfied. Notice that the Masonite is used with its rough side out.

Next I laid the cutout flat and painted it with flat green latex house paint. I let that dry and sprinkled on ground foam as close to the same color as I could find and secured it the same way that Jeff bonded the ballast: a rubbing alcohol spray followed by diluted white glue. See fig. 3. After this had dried, I propped it up, ran a bead of full-strength white glue along the top edge, and added foam to give a very fine ragged edge.

It turned out that the foam I used looked too bright, so I airbrushed on some Floquil Dark Green mix. Later, when the pine tree cutout was added, the hill cutout looked too dark, and it was too similar to the pine color for much contrast. I laid the hill cutout flat again and this time used a squirt bottle to apply diluted pale sea green latex, which is much cheaper than Floquil. The diluted paint softened the white glue, so I kept the Masonite flat until totally dry so the foam wouldn't fall off.

Probably either of the two coloring methods would have been sufficient by itself, but don't be discouraged if at first you don't hit it quite right. I always seem to muddle around until finally I stumble onto the result I'm looking for.

The pine tree cutout just in front of the hill cutout is much the same, but I made the top saw-toothed to match the model trees that would go in front of it — see the second photo in fig. 3. This time I made the mistake of adding the foam to the unpainted cutout, so later I squirted on some dark green latex to color the raw edge and the tips. This color was a little different from the foam color, but I liked the way its vertical streaking broke up the uniformity.

CLOUD PAINTING

I had gotten this far before I screwed up enough courage to tackle the cloud painting with the assistance of Jim Sapienza

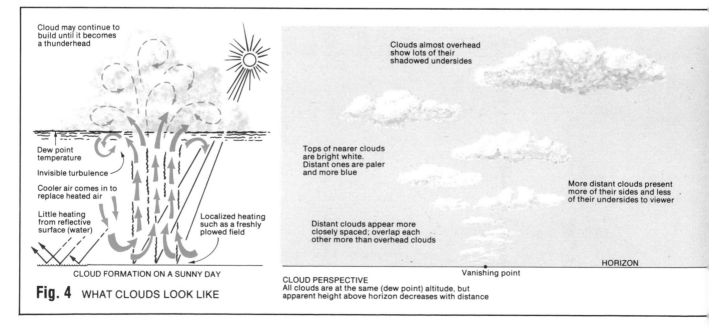

Fig. 4 WHAT CLOUDS LOOK LIKE

CLOUD FORMATION ON A SUNNY DAY

Cloud may continue to build until it becomes a thunderhead

Dew point temperature

Invisible turbulence

Cooler air comes in to replace heated air

Little heating from reflective surface (water)

Localized heating such as a freshly plowed field

Clouds almost overhead show lots of their shadowed undersides

Tops of nearer clouds are bright white. Distant ones are paler and more blue

More distant clouds present more of their sides and less of their undersides to viewer

Distant clouds appear more closely spaced; overlap each other more than overhead clouds

Vanishing point

HORIZON

CLOUD PERSPECTIVE
All clouds are at the same (dew point) altitude, but apparent height above horizon decreases with distance

and Bill Mahaney. First the two Masonite flats were removed, and then I reread the notes left behind by former member Brad Toole, who invented the following techniques and painted all of our clouds to this point.

Let me give you a little theory first. Clouds vary with the weather, but we like to suggest those you'd see on an ideally bright, sunny railfan's day. Figure 4 illustrates what those clouds look like and why. The effects of perspective are important, and I'm including the flying saucer analogy to try to make them clearer. Clouds are not as regular as a flying saucer formation, but I find this analogy helps me to paint them.

We found it difficult to spray cloud shapes with an airbrush, so Brad came up with the idea of using a paint applicator akin to a powder puff (or a Polly Puff). He tore off a chunk of the foam rubber that is used to package brass engines and stapled it to a 3-foot stick of wood. Actually he made two, one to apply just the white and a second for blues and grays.

We use a very white flat latex, the sky blue latex, and a tube of dark brown or gray acrylic artist's color. Mixing just a little of the acrylic with some blue and white makes a shadow color. It has to be mixed thoroughly, as clouds with dark blotches just don't make it. The shadowing adds real punch to the clouds, which look lifeless and dull if painted only with blue and white.

The easiest clouds are the ones high up on the backdrop, or nearly overhead — again, we're assuming all are at the same altitude in the imaginary sky. Figure 5 shows the basic steps for painting clouds. When you try this remember to twist your wrist to avoid repetitious patterns; to use a few big, dramatic pats rather than a fluttering or stuttering motion; and to avoid unnatural shapes. Working some of the blue into the cloud makes it look thinner, while the shadow color makes it look dense. If it's a big cloud, add some shadowing in the higher sections. Practice by

painting a few of the higher clouds first.

Because of the apparent overlap near the horizon, I next went all the way to the bottom of the backdrop and worked up. Instead of using pure white for the lowest (most distant) clouds, I mixed up some white and sky blue. Because our backdrops are so long, we haven't tried to lighten the sky near the horizon. Making the distant clouds bluer compensates for this somewhat, by decreasing the contrast between sky and clouds close to the horizon.

I let these clouds dry until the paint looked flat, then continued by overlapping the next set of clouds. Figure 5 also shows how the clouds should change as they get higher on the backdrop. Having already painted the two extremes of clouds helped me make a smooth transition as I worked my way up the sky.

If you have problems, let the clouds dry thoroughly and paint over them, either patting on bigger clouds or covering them with sky blue. But don't be too hard on yourself. I found that as I painted clouds I studied them too critically, and would be totally discouraged. Going away for at least 15 minutes made them seem much better when I returned.

Clouds should vary a lot in size, from potential thunderheads to slight wisps. On the average, however, the clouds should be scaled down if the backdrop is near the aisle, and scaled up when far back. Also, don't let the clouds dominate the layout, or be so small that they aren't effective.

GRASS MAT FIELDS

There doesn't seem to have been much scenery done with commercial flocked grass papers on advanced model railroads. In this scene, the prototype photo suggested the need for wide expanses of grass, with a very fine, vertical texture. A thick layer of ground foam is too chunky, and a thin layer resembles a golf course, so I took a second look at a roll of grass paper — by Kibri or Vollmer, I don't remember which — we had on hand at the club.

The grass paper had the right texture, but its color variations were on the wrong scale. The fibers were a homogenized mixture of greens and browns, giving a salt-and-pepper appearance up close, but at any distance appearing as a uniform color. Actual wild grass grows in colonies that give a patchy look to the field. Like repainting the marble-colored plastic walls that come in some structure kits, the cure should be obvious.

As when I painted the Masonite flats, I wound up using a two-step process because the first step wasn't completely satisfactory. First of all I cut the grass paper to the shape of the area, then crumpled it and spread it out again. I squirted on diluted grass green latex, thoroughly saturating the paper backing, and positioned it while still wet.

The latex didn't really color the fibers, but it did color the mat, so I squirted on a sandy brown color in spots to suggest areas of thin grass where the soil was showing through a bit. I then added some diluted white glue, and when it was all dry I sprayed the grass with a mixture of Flo-

quil Depot Olive and Mud. By spraying horizontally across the field I was able to color just the fibers.

When dry the fibers were no longer soft, but rigid like a field of little spikes. This proved handy later by providing a Velcro-like attachment for some of the low-lying bushes. Figure 6 shows the grass mat in place, along with the rest of the foliage I added at Summit.

UNLONESOME PINES AND OTHER VEGETATION

After the grass mat was dry, I drilled holes for the commercial bottle-brush pines, using a drill bit slightly larger than the diameter of the wire trunks. I drilled a surplus of holes, just in case, then vacuumed up the sawdust and plaster dust. Sometimes the plaster leaves a white blush that can't be vacuumed away, but squirting on a wash of any natural color — green, brown, gray, or yellow — removes the blush without appreciably changing the scenery color.

The brand (and quality) of the pines is not important. Kibri, Noch, Preiser, and Vollmer all make them, and because we need a lot of them we just buy whichever we can find cheapest. For this particular prototype I wanted trees with a fairly slender profile, and a height of about 4" or less.

My first step is to destroy the trees' symmetry by vigorously attacking them with shears, removing whole chunks of bristles. When I have a respectable pile of trees, I mix up some diluted white glue in a container big enough to dunk a whole tree, and open a bag of AMSI medium or fine dark green foam. I dunk each tree in turn in glue, shake off the excess, roll it in the foam as if breading chicken, then plant it while it's still wet.

While it is possible to "shake-n-bake" a bunch of trees or bushes at the workbench, and plant them when dry, I prefer to make them on the spot and plant them immediately. The wet glue runs down and secures the tree, and if any trees touch they just get glued together.

When dry, any leaning trees can be straightened by bending the wire trunks near the ground. Trees try to grow vertically, and nothing looks funnier than a forest of pines pointing every which way.

As per the prototype, I planted several pines on a little knoll in front of the background row. To make these look much closer, I dusted on some brighter green foam after the dark green. I added a couple of pieces of lichen, also foam covered in the same manner, just behind the standout pines. (Foam-covered lichen dries hard as a rock, but who cares if it isn't soft and cushy? If you pick your own and plan to cover it with foam, I'd leave out the expensive glycerine, using the white glue as a preservative.)

For the line of bushes obscuring the base of the pine row, I used Bill Kennedy's technique of stretching out AHM foliage net, impaling it on the grass mat, spraying with hair spray, and sprinkling on Woodland Scenics blended turf. Little clumps of the same bush in the foreground helped break up the uniform look of the field, as did clumps of stretched-out Woodland Scenics foliage.

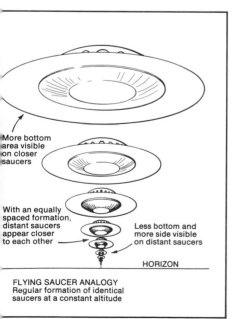

More bottom area visible on closer saucers

With an equally spaced formation, distant saucers appear closer to each other

Less bottom and more side visible on distant saucers

HORIZON

FLYING SAUCER ANALOGY
Regular formation of identical saucers at a constant altitude

HIGH, OVERHEAD CLOUD

Pat on cloud shape with full-strength white

Paint overhead clouds first

Pat on shadow color to suggest three-dimensional shape

Paint distant clouds next, then work up backdrop painting intermediate clouds

Whiteness increases more rapidly than spacing or size as clouds get higher on the backdrop

A SKY FULL OF CLOUDS

Fig. 5 PAINTING CLOUDS

DISTANT, LOW CLOUD

Pat on cloud shape with blue and white mixture

Add blue to shadow color and pat on, smearing sideways to make bottom outline hazy and indistinc

I made a few clumps of taller grass with strands of fake fur embedded in little puddles of white glue. Since the synthetic fibers of the fake fur are nearly impossible to dye, I colored some with diluted latex and others with a spray of Floquil. You can also find similar fibers in a variety of natural grass greens, sold for making fishing lures.

Fake fur comes in various naps, but you may not always find all variations in one store. We have been using material that has fibers a couple of inches long. As we cut off ¼" clumps, the piece winds up with a shag cut, at which point the whole swatch can be planted. As with the grass paper, foliage has to be planted to disguise the edges.

Because the depth of the scene is so condensed, I planted all the vegetation in long narrow patches, roughly parallel to the track. It's important to clump the different materials in colonies of irregular sizes, rather than a single clump of this next to a clump of that.

Jeff English added the signal line poles he built from N&G kits. Future detailing will include a beaver-dammed pond, as soon as we find a good picture of a beaver dam, tucked away in one corner.

The nice thing about this technique of working directly from pictures is that Mother Nature has done all the work of planning and tests her plans by building a model in a nice large scale, so we can see beforehand what it will look like on our layout. What could be simpler? ✿

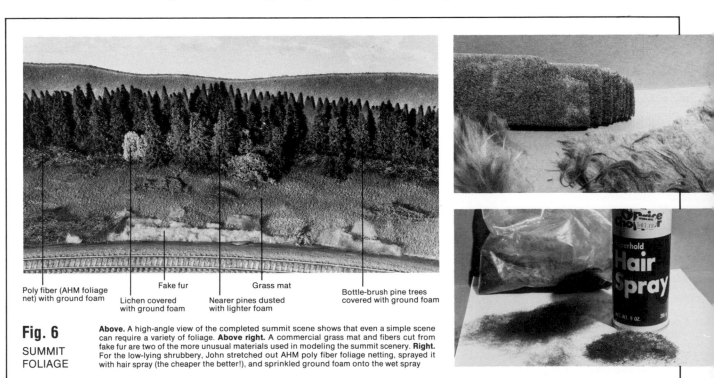

Poly fiber (AHM foliage net) with ground foam

Lichen covered with ground foam

Fake fur

Nearer pines dusted with lighter foam

Grass mat

Bottle-brush pine trees covered with ground foam

Fig. 6
SUMMIT
FOLIAGE

Above. A high-angle view of the completed summit scene shows that even a simple scene can require a variety of foliage. **Above right.** A commercial grass mat and fibers cut from fake fur are two of the more unusual materials used in modeling the summit scenery. **Right.** For the low-lying shrubbery, John stretched out AHM poly fiber foliage netting, sprayed it with hair spray (the cheaper the better!), and sprinkled ground foam onto the wet spray

Cloud painting for the summit scene underway. We see three containers holding blue-white, white, and shadow-gray paint; one foam applicator for the white paint and one for mixed colors; and a prototype photo for handy reference

Here's Alco S-4 switcher no. 1270 working the Woods River yard. The boards between the foreground rails cover a Kadee electromagnetic uncoupling ramp. The handcar marks the ramp's center. The phone box follows B&M practice, as do the switch stands with rectangular targets.

Weathering your yards

Most prototype yards
are eyesores, so why shouldn't yours be too?

BY PAUL J. DOLKOS
PHOTOS BY THE AUTHOR

WE MODEL RAILROADERS love our yards. On many layouts they are the centerpiece. The Woods River yard on my Boston & Maine layout is about 10 feet long with seven parallel tracks. It holds about 80 cars on the classification tracks. There are two tracks for arrivals and departures.

As I worked on it I really looked forward to its completion. I put a light cosmetic curve in it such as those found in yards that bend along a river bank. I varied the tie coloring, painted the rails, and neatly spread the cinder ballast. Voila! The masterpiece was complete.

But what a letdown. It worked fine, but it really didn't look as great as I had imagined it would; it was kind of dull. But then maybe seven parallel tracks don't have that much visual potential.

Then I looked at a prototype yard in my city. The very things that make these facilities the neighborhood eyesore and the bane of city beautifiers were

what was missing in mine. Ballast materials varied, and it was dirty. There was spillage from a variety of loads. There was trash, and grass and weeds were growing here and there. The place was a mess.

So I messed up my new yard. I proceeded with the same trepidation that you have when you take your weathering brush to your newly painted locomotive.

Some sources of yard weathering or texturing that I observed included the following:

● Spillage of cargo such as coal, ce-

Above. The author used a wide variety of textures and colors for his yard weathering. In the foreground is a pile of dirt representing spillage. Soil was washed onto the track in the left background and ground foam was scattered around to represent grass and weeds. **Above.** Soil and gray ballast sprinkled between the tracks contrast with the basic cinder ballast. The telephone box marks the location of concealed uncoupling ramps.

ment, ore, copper, gravel, and grain.

● Oil drippings. Hopefully these are from rolling stock bearings and turnout lubrication, not from tank cars.

● Trash, including paper, chunks of wood, and metal banding.

● Vegetation. Include a variety of colors and heights, dead and alive.

● Ballast in many variations due to reballasting, tie replacement, raising of a rail.

● Soil as opposed to or in lieu of ballast, from erosion, road grades, construction.

I avoided littering the yard with rail sections or loose ties. While they certainly may be present during a maintenance project, the areas where switchmen walk are generally kept clear of such objects. A crewman could easily trip over them, especially at night. So keep safety in mind when you litter your yard.

The materials I used for my yard weathering were much the same as those you would use on any scenery project. For spillage I used crushed materials such as rock ballast, sand, or sifted dirt, as long as the color contrasted with the cinder ballast. You should vary the spillage patterns too. Materials leaking from hoppers tend to drop between the rails, while from boxcars they drop outside the rails. Drippings are probably best done with paint. For trash use whatever turns up; although, I must confess I really haven't thrown little scraps of paper around my yard yet. The vegetation can be ground foam or tufts of rope or carpeting.

I did not weather all tracks equally. The arrival and departure tracks I left relatively clean on the theory that perhaps they receive a little more maintenance. But the track in the back that most likely would be used for dead car storage is covered with vegetation and soil washed down an adjacent embankment (nobody takes care of the drainage ditches). Between these two extremes there is the normal spillage and a few weeds. This variation is just another way of providing a range of contrast to add more interest.

I also found that yard weathering could be used to mark the location of under-the-track Kadee uncoupling ramps. A patch of grass, a tuft of weeds can be distinctive, yet unobtrusive when nothing else seems right for a marker. The plastic yard limit signs that come with the ramps aren't appropriate in the middle of the yard.

Yard weathering is something you should do in stages. Grow a little grass, spill a little coal, pile up some dirt. Stand back and see what you think. Add litter as the mood suits. After all that eyesore railroad yard in your town didn't get to be that way all in one day either. The railroad might have even taken some nice public relations pictures of the yard when they opened it long ago showing how nice it was. Yards just don't stay that way. ♦

Pathways to detail

Plaster sidewalks for plastic people

BY JOHN NEHRICH
PHOTOS BY THE AUTHOR

BEFORE the automobile most people walked; hence, the sidewalks were as important to personal mobility as the streets that paralleled them. The sidewalks I'll describe are typical of those found in upstate New York (Troy), but the principles of design, modeling, and detailing are similar for any area.

The most primitive sidewalk is a line of curbstones with a bare dirt path cut through the grass about 5 feet in from the road. The next step up is a row of variously shaded slate slabs of constant width but of varied length. The slabs are often tilted due to settling of the ground, frost heaves, and the upward thrust of growing tree roots. Brick, wood, gravel, blacktop, and other materials, including marble (in Vermont), have all been used for sidewalk paving. Each type requires different modeling techniques.

The most common sidewalk material at present is concrete. See fig. 1. The concrete is poured in place between formers, with expansion cracks dividing it up into a regular grid pattern. In the Troy area sidewalks in the business district are usually two squares wide, with the squares nearest the street forming the splash zone. See fig. 2.

One-square-wide sidewalks are normally only found in crowded industrial and residential areas. In outlying areas the splash zone may be grass. Brick laid in a herring-bone pattern has also been used. Old or badly maintained concrete may be extensively cracked or even totally disintegrated in spots. Some areas may be repaired with blacktop. See figs. 1 and 2. These features all serve to randomize the regular grid pattern — a helpful feature in scale modeling.

A sidewalk is normally about 4″ above the surrounding street, sloping up and

The foliage growing in the cracks in this plaster sidewalk on the Rensselaer club layout is ground foam attached with white glue. Clumps of fake fur can also be used sparingly.

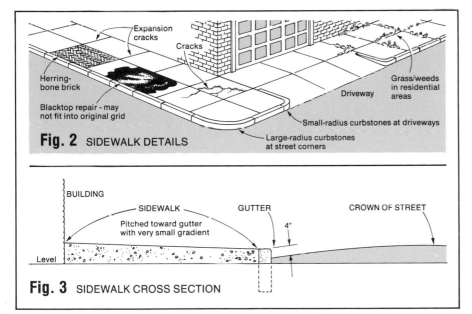

Fig. 2 SIDEWALK DETAILS

- Expansion cracks
- Cracks
- Herring-bone brick
- Blacktop repair - may not fit into original grid
- Driveway
- Grass/weeds in residential areas
- Small-radius curbstones at driveways
- Large-radius curbstones at street corners

Fig. 3 SIDEWALK CROSS SECTION

- BUILDING
- SIDEWALK
- Pitched toward gutter with very small gradient
- Level
- GUTTER
- 4"
- CROWN OF STREET

Fig. 1. A representative sidewalk in my community consists of concrete squares well patched with asphalt, and it has grass and weeds growing up through the expansion joints.

away from the street, so rainwater drains into the gutter. See fig. 3.

Curbstones are just that — stone — often granite, about 4″ wide and a foot deep, with about 4″ extending above street level. Each curbstone is up to 4 feet long, and the joints do not necessarily coincide with those of the sidewalk grid. The curbstones curve around corners, and it is a sign of contemporary times when they dip at pedestrian crossings for wheelchair access. Curbstones are omitted at driveway locations.

Growing vegetation can exert an unbelievable hydraulic pressure to force its way between any sidewalk cracks. See fig. 1 again.

Excessive trampling limits its growth in areas of heavy pedestrian traffic, but sidewalks off the beaten path become extensively foliated.

MODELING SIDEWALKS

On the Rensselaer Model Railroad Society's HO club layout, most of the sidewalks are the poured concrete type. For sidewalks set back from the viewing aisles, we use the plastic sidewalks that come with Heljan and other injection molded structure kits. The pieces are affixed with Walthers Goo and brush-painted with Floquil White mixed 50:50 with either Earth, Concrete, Grime, Driftwood, or Reefer Gray to kill the raw plastic look. The exact color is not important, but you want an off-white or dirty white. To hide any gaps along the gutter where the sidewalk isn't quite flat, brush a layer of finely sifted dirt up to the sidewalk edge and affix it with diluted white glue.

For sidewalks that are subject to close scrutiny, we use a poured-plaster technique. See the model photo. First, glue down a line of prepainted curbstones — Evergreen styrene .040″-square strip cut into ½″-long pieces (wood strips can also be used). The curb color should be the same as the sidewalk.

Spoon a thick mix of plaster into the area between building and curb, and then scrape the top surface with the blade of a trowel or putty knife held vertically. A piece of styrene or other hard material will also work. Use the curb as a guide. You can use a second slightly taller runner positioned along the building itself as a guide for the other side of the scraping blade. If necessary, sand the plaster when dry in order to obtain a smooth surface.

After the plaster has set, carve it into 4- to 5-foot squares using a straightedge and a common sharp scriber. The exact dimension is not important, but maintain that dimension over the area. Carve some cracks freehand, and paint the surface the same paint mix as the curbstones. Add a few asphalt patches using a dark gray (but not black) color. Follow the basic coloring with a wash of dilute black (acrylic paint, India ink, coffee, etc.). For the grass plots around the sidewalks we use a mix of several materials including electrostatic grass (Boyd), grass paper (avoid the emerald green type), clumps of appropriately colored fake fur, and different grades and colors of ground foam.

To foliate the sidewalk, we apply little dabs of white glue along the cracks, sprinkle on Woodland Scenics Turf, and then gently blow away the excess. This technique works as well on the plastic sidewalks as it does on the plaster ones. A clump of fake fur, used sparingly, here and there along a crack can be used for contrast. Vary the degree of foliage to simulate the character of the sidewalk and the neighborhood it serves. ✿

Sheridan, Colorado: 1927

With the help of a mirror, you can create the
illusion of a good-size mining town in only 5 square feet

BY MALCOLM FURLOW
PHOTOS BY THE AUTHOR

THROUGH the mist that envelopes the snow-capped peaks of the San Juans there is evidence of man's existence in this beautiful, but harsh, place. Born as a mining camp in 1875, Sheridan has experienced enormous wealth — and depressing poverty. Its colorful past is one of hardrock miners, Ute Indians, men sporting high Stetson hats and madams that whistle from the high balconies along Front Street.

The Indians ruled over the land until the late 1800s, living in the valleys between the high peaks. Hunting was good, water was plentiful, and the weather was cool in the summer. But, with the discovery of gold in 1860, the Indians began to disappear from the high grassy mesa. The Wild West was truly unfolding! The prospectors, with their life's possessions on their wagons, or on their horses, or even on their backs came in search of the yellow ore that would make them rich!

Early prospectors to the area gazed in wonderment at the beautiful panorama unfolding before their eyes: the rugged, majestic mountains rising to 14,000 feet in the distance; the sparkling mountain streams cascading along, eventually forming Chama Creek and the lake the Ute Indians call Shananaux. It was, and still is, a beautiful area.

The Denver & Rio Chama Western RR staked its claim to the town early and sent its slim gauge rails snaking their way through Silver Canyon, with the roaring waters of Chama Creek nipping at the ribbons of steel. Every spring the waters of Chama Creek rise and threaten to swallow the roadbed, and actually have on several occasions.

In April of 1862 the Colorado Territorial Legislature recognized the area in and around Sheridan and organized the region into Findley County.

Colonel Findley was one of the early prospectors to the area and founder of the rich Findley Mine at the base of Sheridan Peak. He later became the first mayor of Sheridan.

In 1875, as the rumor of still richer strikes along the base of Sheridan Mountain spread throughout Colorado, newcomers flooded the area, settling in makeshift frame housing or tents. Sawmills ran night and day to supply the burgeoning town with enormous amounts of timber for construction. By 1878 more than 400 buildings stood in a place that had been pastureland only 3 years earlier.

Snow and cold were serious problems for the early settlers of Sheridan. Every winter deep snowdrifts blocked the toll road leading out of the city, and the Black Bear and Deadman slides would run, covering the tracks of the Rio Chama with tons of snow, fallen timbers, and debris. Even during mild winters, the mines could ship out concentrates only a few times, and getting supplies in from Silverton or Durango required that the Silver Canyon tracks be plowed out with the D & RCW's rotary on a regular basis.

Today (1927), the mines around Sheridan are all but shut down. Despite the lack of ore shipments from the major gold mines of the area, the little diamond-stacked Consolidations of the Rio Chama still make an occasional run up Silver Canyon to Sheridan. Their mournful whistles reverberate off the canyon walls as they pull their consists along the rusty right-of-way. And, though the mining of high-grade ore has slipped into a long depression, the folks of Sheridan cling to the idea that a rebirth of their industry is just around the mountain.

THE reason I've included this fictitious history of Sheridan (not to be confused with the real city of Sheridan, Colo., a suburb of Denver) was to give you an idea of the thinking that went into the building of the model town on my Denver & Rio Chama Western.

I wanted Sheridan to represent a town that had started life as a mining camp, later becoming a "boom town," and finally, a depressed area in the late 1920s. The community had passed its time of maximum growth and was declining in population. As the automobile began to invade Colorado, better roads were built, and some cities began to realize that any future prosperity would have to come from the tourist trade. On the Rio Chama, however, Sheridan is forever locked in the past — 1927 to be exact.

Before I could start building, I needed to see what was required to develop a "1927 Colorado small-town atmosphere." A trip through Colorado last summer provided a wealth of information on what a town like the one I wanted to model might look like. I took numerous photos and gathered as much information as I could. A trip to Central City, Colo. (Victor is even better for study purposes), really gives the modeler insight into what these towns must have been like in their heyday. My family and I were entranced by those quaint old vintage buildings resting on their stone footings, and by the stone and timber retaining walls lining almost every street.

Some of these little villages grew out of the original boom towns. Often hastily built out of wood, most of them experienced devastating fires that quickly demanded the use of stouter materials such as brick or stone. Built on the up-and-down world of Colorado, these mining towns had real charm. From their false fronts to their wooden-planked walkways, they added a certain gracefulness to the Wild West.

MIRRORS

The space actually taken up by Sheridan on my layout is quite small. Most of the structures are small so as not to overpower other areas surrounding the city. The town seems larger than it is because it was built against a mirror to effectively expand the scene. Through careful blending of structures and scenery materials placed up against the mirror, and actually painting some scenery on the mirror surface, the technique can be quite effective.

The mirror must be placed so the viewer is unable to see his reflection in it. The late John Allen used mirrors skillfully on his legendary Gorre & Daphetid. A study of the placement of mirrors on John Allen's layout reveals that the mirrors were sometimes placed at angles not exactly perpendicular to the wall, and in some instances were angled to the right or left. John apparently

Wall

Backdrop

3-D scenery

Keep this end against
(use as a pivot p[...])

Buildings and
trees can be
glued to mirror
or painted on

Mirror

Mirror can be
turned away 1 c
2 inches from th[...]
end to pick up [...]
of 3-D scenery

Construction of Sheridan began with the assembly of a short section of L-girder framework. The base for the main road was cut from plain cardboard and taped in position. The line drawing above shows how the mirror was positioned and a few of the tricks the author used to effectively blend the mirror into the scene. Some scenery can be painted on the mirror and a few trees with half a trunk can be glued to the mirror.

reasoned that this type of placement would catch more of the existing scenery and lessen the possibility of the viewer seeing himself.

Any signs or writing displayed on the building must not show up in the mirror unless the printing is backwards (a mirror image). The sides of buildings being reflected by the mirror can be painted a different color than the rest of the structure.

This little trick, along with printing the signs backwards, will create the illusion of many different buildings all crowded together. I even painted a car yellow on one side and green on the other to make it look

as though there were two different cars in the scene. Trees with half a trunk can be attached to the mirror, creating a three-dimensional effect. Another neat trick is to place a building under construction next to the mirror.

A surface-reflection (first-surface) mirror is the best kind to use, but they are expensive. Also, surface mirrors are quite fragile, and the surface itself scratches very easily. Ordinary looking glass (second-surface) mirrors work okay even though there is a slight space (a layer of glass) between where the three-dimensional scenery meets the actual mirrored surface.

Mirrors, especially in the corner areas of the railroad, will be an integral part of my Rio Chama as it grows.

PLANNING

As stated before, the space available for Sheridan was exceptionally small for the effect I was seeking. The measurements I made before beginning construction proved that things would be very tight, and a careful scrutiny of the track I wanted to run into the area was required. I wanted avenues for possible expansion, as well as space for the branch line to be completed in the future.

Left. The next step was casting the retaining walls using latex rubber molds. These castings were applied wet to the hardshell base. Center. Attention was then focused on background scenery. Grocery-bag paper was crumpled up and taped to the wall and to the mirror. These shapes were studied awhile before proceeding. Right. This is how the area looked much later. A foundation is being added for another structure.

Left to right. The mirror was installed and some structures were temporarily positioned to see how their reflections looked. Furlow formed a rugged hardshell base using strips of grocery-bag paper dipped in Hydrocal plaster. After the hardshell was completed, the building foundation castings were glued in position. The structures were temporarily placed on their foundations and checked to see if they were level.

In addition to railroad track, roads serving Sheridan had to be plotted. I wanted the winding, twisting, mountain-type dirt roads of Colorado. I reasoned that the main road leading into Sheridan would have to start low and progressively twist and wind through town to a higher elevation, skirt through a small canyon, and finally disappear into the backdrop. This would give the viewer an uncluttered look at Sheridan and establish the reason for the sloping real estate and numerous retaining walls. I jotted down all of these ideas on pieces of paper so I could study the plan later on and so I wouldn't forget any.

CONSTRUCTION

Construction of Sheridan began with the assembly of a short section of L-girder framework measuring 2'-0" x 2'-6". I attached it between the existing wall facing the layout and the end of the railroad. This section was designed to be removable, as were all other sections of the Rio Chama, in case I have to move or want to change the layout. The steps in the construction are shown in the photos and explained briefly in the captions.

The main road base I cut out of cardboard (regular box-type cardboard) and positioned on the benchwork. Following a session of "cut and fit," I had finally tailored the roads to the small space and had cut risers to elevate the roadbed and determine the grade as shown on the photo.

The fact that the buildings in my model town are built on different levels allows me to take full advantage of the visual gains made by foundations at different heights. Not only does varying the height of the foundations add realism, it also helps keep the eye moving through the scene, thus achieving a "busy" look. I also varied the construction materials for the foundations, including stone, brick, and wood.

Left. The foundation for the additional structure is completed. Center. Ruts were carved in the roads using an X-Acto knife before the plaster was completely set up. Right photo. The author's attention to detail goes beyond ground level. Notice the puddles of water on the flat roofs. The lower roof on the building in the foreground has some water and even a pile of broken glass. There's also a broom handy for the cleanup.

But first I cut subfoundations for the buildings from cardstock and taped them down at predetermined sites along the roadway. I gave some of these subfoundations added support from underneath and, using hardshell terrain, formed a rigid base for the buildings. To shape the hardshell, I dip strips of grocery-bag paper into a soupy mix of Hydrocal plaster and drape them over the cardboard forms.

I temporarily left the scenery in the Hydrocal stage and focused my attention on the structures and how they would fit their respective foundations. Some of the buildings were kitbashed to fit a given area, while others were designed and finished before the subfoundations were installed. That is to say, the foundations were fitted to the already finished building. As I see it, that's the most efficient method.

The Palace Hotel, on the other hand, was designed around an already existing multi-level foundation. This was accomplished using castings from a Magnuson Models hotel kit and redoing the ends and sides to match the foundation. The end of the building containing the drugstore was made from a plaster casting taken from a latex mold and joined to the Magnuson castings with epoxy cement. Some detail parts, such as roof trim, were removed with a motor tool for use at other locations or to conceal unwanted seams where two sides came together.

The Argonaut Building had its beginning as a Magnuson Miners Union Hall. I cut it down in length, as well as width, to fit on its previously constructed foundation. I plan to add both interior and exterior lights to all the structures at some future time. A few street lights will be installed also. The structures are removable so that I can add more detailing later.

The roads running through Sheridan are primarily decomposed granite, sifted to a sand-like consistency, and secured with a white glue and water mix. As the photos show, ruts can be darkened a little using acrylic colors a shade darker than the surrounding road surface. The upper ridge of the rut can be dry-brushed with a color that's a shade lighter than the road surface. This will highlight the roadway and make it seem to be what it really is — a dirt road.

Puddles of water can be simulated with white glue, or model airplane cement, or epoxy cement. Weeds can be added on the road surface and along the edges of the road. Good materials for simulating weeds are rope fibers and cattails. The cattails can be pulled apart and glued in place for a really scale-looking weed.

Signs play an important part in this type of scene, and I must confess I'm a sign freak. Although there already are numerous signs in and around Sheridan, more will be added later. Most of the sign lettering was done using dry transfers.

A small-town scene can be added to and upgraded continously. I find myself going back over Sheridan frequently, as new ideas for detail pop into my head.

The creation of Sheridan has been totally enjoyable from its conception, through field study in Colorado, to its actual construction. I hope this article will encourage some of you to research a town or two and begin construction. I think you'll find it's fun, as well as an educational experience. ✿

Mini-mirrors

They reflect more light than scenery

BY JOHN NEHRICH
PHOTOS BY THE AUTHOR

In this higher-than-normal view, the pencil points to the small mirror John Nehrich used to light up the end of Summit Road on the Berkshire Lines. The photos below show the normal viewing angle.

CLOSE to the backdrop, scenery gets compressed. We model the foreground in full, but farther back we forshorten hills, simulate mountains with flats, and represent miles and miles of atmosphere in but the thickness of a coat of paint.

When supposedly separate objects are packed close together, there is no place for their shadows to fall except one on another. The area of a shadow is related to how tall an object is, and height doesn't fall off as fast as depth in most model railroad scenery. That's how we wind up with caves of shadows next to the backdrop.

We could attempt to eliminate these with small lamps, but they'd have to be color- and intensity-balanced with the ambient lighting, and rebalanced for floodlit photography. A mirror, on the other hand, automatically matches the room lighting, neatly solving the problem of color balance.

It was John Allen who took mirrors out of the fun house and onto the layout, showing how a strategically placed mirror can double a scene. He made it seem easy, so gracefully did he arrange the various elements to work in reflection — see the "The art of using mirrors" in the December 1981 MR. However, the prototype is not always so accommodating as to be symmetric around a plane, and so this technique rarely works when trying to copy specific prototype scenes.

On the Rensselaer Model Railroad Society's club railroad, the New England, Berkshire & Western, we are using mirrors in small doses, and more for their ability to reflect light than to reflect objects. In fact the mirror itself need not even show. It can be just around the bend in a road, for instance, and still reflect light to eliminate the effect of looking into a dark cave in the scenery.

In the example here, the mirror is just at the edge of visibility. That means that you needn't fuss about having a perfect reflection. The mirror can be the ordinary back-silvered type, instead of the special front-silvered mirrors desirable for John Allen's technique. I stuck the mirror into the road scene as an afterthought, and could just as easily have pulled it back out if it hadn't worked. From normal viewing angles the mirror does not reflect any more road than you can see without it, but it does light up the "tunnel."

In trying to cut down an automobile rear-view mirror, I wound up with a jagged edge, but that helps camouflage the top of the mirror. The mirror is supported by nothing but the entangling foliage. Baby's breath, from florists' or craft stores, helps disguise the sides of the mirror, as you can see through it only partially. It comes in different degrees of laciness, so keep looking if the first bouquets you see are too coarse.

Under a bridge, around the corner of a building, any place where you wish you had light instead of shadows, try using a mini-mirror. ☼

Summit Road, before. Look just above the tender of Kyle Williams' 2-8-0 and you'll see the road bending into a shadowy cave near the backdrop.

After the mirror is in place, the light that it reflects makes Summit Road seem to extend into the distance rather than disappear into a tunnel.

An SP local freight rolls through a Sonoran desert pass. The large saguaro, ocotillo, and shrubs of this desert provide a striking setting for this western railroad.

Modeling the great American deserts

The wastelands can make beautiful and fascinating scenery for your layout

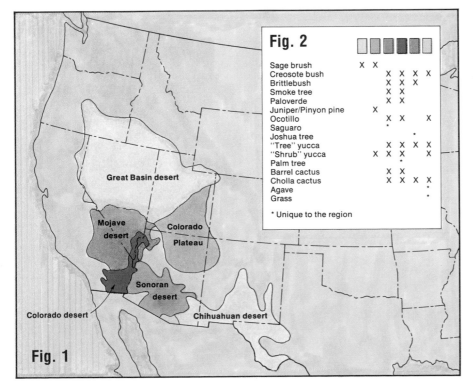

Fig. 2

Sage brush	X	X				
Creosote bush			X	X	X	X
Brittlebush			X	X	X	
Smoke tree			X	X		
Paloverde			X	X		
Juniper/Pinyon pine	X					
Ocotillo			X	X		X
Saguaro			*			
Joshua tree				*		
"Tree" yucca			X	X	X	X
"Shrub" yucca	X	X	X			X
Palm tree			*			
Barrel cactus			X	X		
Cholla cactus			X	X	X	X
Agave						*
Grass						*

* Unique to the region

BY MARK JUNGE
PHOTOS BY THE AUTHOR

I HAVE nothing against forests and mountains, but sometimes I long for the wide-open spaces of the desert. It's a varied land of sculptured rocks, bizarre plants, and blazing springtime color. Contrary to what you might think, desert scenery makes a great setting for a model railroad, and it's not all that difficult to model. But, as with most any project, there are a few things you need to know before getting started.

The American desert can be divided into distinct regions, from four to six depending on whom you talk to. Each region has a distinct look to it, so by carefully choosing the plants you model, you can establish the general locale of your railroad. Refer to the map (fig. 1), the chart (fig. 2), and the photos of the dioramas I built for each of the regions.

Two things should be mentioned with regard to the map. First, the boundaries between these regions are not as clear cut as the map makes them appear. One region gradually blends into another. Thus, where the Mojave meets the Sonoran desert, you'll find plants characteristic of both regions.

Second, the regions as I've modeled them are somewhat idealized. The pictures show

Fig. 1

Great Basin desert

Mojave desert

Colorado Plateau

Colorado desert

Sonoran desert

Chihuahuan desert

Great Basin desert: rather drab, with sagebrush and other small shrubs

scenery typical of the regions, but that doesn't mean that *all* of the region shown looks that way. Many areas of the Colorado, Sonoran, and Chihuahuan deserts, for example, have nothing but creosote bush, with none of the more characteristic plants present.

Therefore, if you're modeling a specific prototype in the Southwest, do a little research to find out what the scenery actually looks like in the area you're interested in. Enough school. Let's get to work!

TREES AND SHRUBS

Even the driest deserts in North America have some sort of shrubbery, so this is a good place to start. I prefer to use lichen rather than ground foam to represent desert trees and shrubs, which are more open than their counterparts growing in wetter regions. I used Campbell's Gray Lichen, using some as it is, and dyeing some in shades of gray-green and olive-green.

I made the dye by mixing Liquitex acrylic paint in a container of enough water to submerge the lichen. These are the approximate proportions of paint I used for making dyes:

● Gray-green — 2 parts cadmium yellow, 2 parts ultramarine blue, 1 part black, 1 part white.

● Olive-green — 4 parts cadmium yellow, 2 parts ultramarine blue, 2 parts black, 1 part white.

● Scorch — 2 parts oxide, 1 part cadmium yellow, 1 part black, 1 part white. (This color will be needed only if you're making smoke trees).

Simply soak the lichen in the dye, squeeze out the excess, and set it aside to dry. When you're ready to use it, cut or rip the lichen to the sizes and shapes you'll need, as illustrated in fig. 3.

Pieces of the gray-green and olive-green lichen can be used as is to represent 2- to 3-foot-high shrubs commonly found in all of the desert regions. Sagebrush is made from gray-green lichen airbrushed lightly with Floquil Concrete, then separated into 2-foot-high pieces. Brittlebush is 1- to 2-foot chunks of gray-green lichen covered with yellow flower material. Use Woodland Scenics yellow flowers or, better yet, dye the flower material a golden yellow, about the color of a Kodak film box. Glue on the flowers with dilute matte medium from a spray bottle used for misting house plants.

Creosote bush, about 4 feet high, is olive-green lichen dusted with Woodland Scenics Turf, again glued with matte medium. Smoke trees, 10 to 12 feet high, are made with gray-green and scorch lichen glued to a twig or painted wire armature.

Paloverde trees are made the same way as smoke trees, using olive-green lichen in place of the gray-green and scorch. Airbrush the entire tree, including the limbs

and trunk, with Floquil Depot Olive. For a paloverde in bloom, spray the tree with dilute matte medium from a spray bottle. Then dust heavily with yellow flowers. These trees can reach 25 feet in height.

Incidentally, the shrubbery need not appear as sparse as I made it for the photos. There are many places in the desert where the ground is barely visible because of the thick shrubbery. Generally, however, you'll want to give the shrubs a lot of elbow room, especially the creosote bushes.

Junipers and pinyon pines can be found in higher elevations of all desert mountains and are common in many areas of the Colorado Plateau. These small trees, about 10 feet high, are made from twigs or by twisting stranded wire into a tree-like shape (either upright or sprawled across the ground) and soldering. Apply Floquil Primer (or light gray paint, if you used nonmetallic trees); when the paint has dried, brush on Floquil Natural Pine stain. In this case, ground foam makes a good fo-

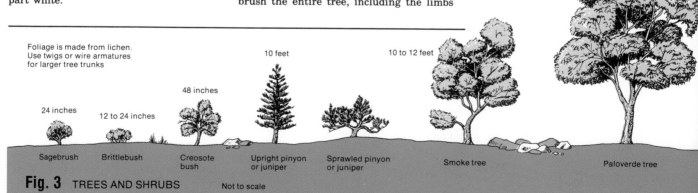

Foliage is made from lichen. Use twigs or wire armatures for larger tree trunks

Up to 25 feet

24 inches — Sagebrush

12 to 24 inches — Brittlebush

48 inches — Creosote bush

10 feet — Upright pinyon or juniper

Sprawled pinyon or juniper

10 to 12 feet — Smoke tree

Paloverde tree

Fig. 3 TREES AND SHRUBS   Not to scale

Colorado desert: a blaze of color with ocotillo, brittlebush, and yucca   Sonoran desert: blooming saguaro cactus and flowering paloverde

liage material, rather than lichen. Use Woodland Scenics Dark Green for pinyon pines and light green for junipers.

OCOTILLO

Ocotillos (fig. 4) are easy to make. Start with wire a scale ¾" to 1" thick. Cut sections 15 to 20 feet long, bunch them together, and solder at one end. Spread and kink the wires, and then clean with soap and warm water. When it has dried, apply Floquil Primer. Next, paint it with Floquil Depot Olive, leaving the first 1 to 2 feet from the base of the plant gray. Coat the wires with matte medium and dust with Woodland Scenics Turf. For flowers, apply Woodland Scenics red flowers at the tips of the wires.

SAGUARO AND BARREL CACTUS

I basically followed John Olson's technique for making these cacti [MR Oct 1982]. Use ¼" balsa for HO; adjust accordingly for other scales. To make a saguaro (fig. 5), cut a piece of balsa to a scale 30 to 40 feet (or shorter, for a younger, armless saguaro), and whittle it into a rounded cylinder, slightly tapered at both ends, and round at the top. The arms are made by gluing short pieces of balsa together and shaping them with a hobby knife. Score vertical grooves in the pieces with a razor saw, then glue the arms to the trunk 15 to 25 feet above ground level.

Paint the cactus with Floquil Roof Brown; when the paint has dried thoroughly, dry-brush the cactus with Depot Olive. Flowers can be made from any small dried flower, caspia buds, or whatever you can find. I used dried star flowers after pulling the petals off, leaving a tiny cup. Paint the outside Depot Olive, the edges white, and the center yellow. Drill holes near the apex of the branches and trunk, insert the flowers, and glue. Saguaros are common on or near foothills; few grow on the drier flats.

Barrel cacti are made the same way (also fig. 5). Carve a 3- to 8-foot section of balsa (¼" for HO) into a barrel shape. You could also use a scale barrel, such as Campbell's wooden barrels, and sand off the "metal" bands. Score vertical grooves and paint the same way as the saguaros. Flowers are arranged along the top rim of the "barrel" as a crown. Proceed as with the saguaro flowers, but paint these flowers yellow for a Colorado desert barrel cactus, or orange or red for a Sonoran desert cactus. Barrel cacti can be set on your layout individually or in clusters. They often tend to lean towards the south, so here's your chance to give your layout a sense of direction!

JOSHUA TREE AND YUCCA

Joshua trees and yuccas (fig. 6) are made from chinelle, available at your local crafts store. Chinelle looks like a big pipe cleaner, except chinelle isn't fuzzy, and it's bigger in diameter than a pipe cleaner. Chinelle is about the right size for S scale. O and HO scalers can use it without concern; N scale modelers should use pipe cleaners.

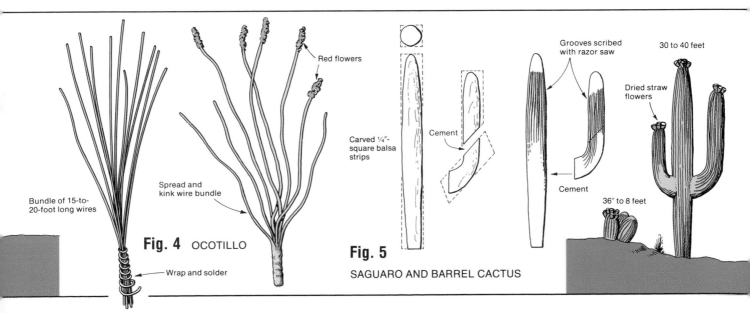

Bundle of 15-to-20-foot long wires
Spread and kink wire bundle
Red flowers
Fig. 4 OCOTILLO
Wrap and solder

Carved ¼"-square balsa strips
Cement
Fig. 5
SAGUARO AND BARREL CACTUS
Grooves scribed with razor saw
Cement
30 to 40 feet
Dried straw flowers
36" to 8 feet

Mojave desert: high desert with grotesquely contorted Joshua trees. (Center) Chihuahuan desert: grass, agave, ocotillo

Start by cutting the chinelle into sections and pulling or shaving away the fibers from the wire at one end where the leaf cluster attaches to a branch or the ground, and at the other end if you're modeling flowers. Apply acetone to the wire stem; this will soften the plastic fibers. Bend the fibers as shown in fig. 6. (I omitted this step when I made the Joshua trees in the color photo; in the future, I intend to bend the fibers for Joshua trees too.)

Airbrush the leaf clusters with Floquil Depot Olive. The lower third of leaf clusters being used for Joshua trees and "tree" yuccas should be airbrushed straw-yellow or yellow-brown. I used UP Armour Yellow mixed with a little Roof Brown. Build up the flowering stalk portions with matte medium or modeling putty. When dry, apply matte medium and cover with Woodland Scenics white flowers. When thoroughly dry, brush on a thin wash of pale yellow, such as Liquitex white with a touch of yellow added.

The tree parts of Joshua trees and "tree" yuccas come from natural twigs, wire armatures, or Woodland Scenics metal trees. The trunk can be straight or forked, up to 30 feet for Joshua trees and 6 feet for "tree" yuccas. Branches on Joshua trees can point in almost any direction, although most should point up. If possible, drill holes in the ends of the branches to accept the cleared wire stems of the chinelle leaf clusters. Paint the trunk and branches a light gray, or with Primer if you used metal trees. When dry, apply a thin wash of Floquil Natural Pine stain. Cement the chinelle sections to the limbs with ACC.

PALM TREE

Fan palms (fig. 7) take a little time and work, but it's worth it. Start with plastic ivy plants. I used Swedish ivy, but others will also work. The leaf clusters simply pull off of the stems. I preferred to cut notches into the leaves, although you could use them as they are. You'll need 4 to 5 clusters for each of

the trees you make. Paint these Depot Olive.

I make the trunk from a dowel, about a scale 2 feet in diameter, regardless of height — palm trunks don't thicken much with age. They can be up to 50 feet tall. (They get taller than that, but unless your layout is huge, they might look out of place.) Cover the trunk with dead fronds (leaves) made of short pieces of jute twine that has been frayed at one end.

Cut off a stem from the plastic ivy, drill a hole in the top of the trunk, and glue the stem in the hole. Push 4 or 5 of the leaf clusters into the stem; these may be glued, but I didn't find it necessary.

I found it advantageous to decide in advance which leaf clusters would go on the bottom and the top of the stack. Before painting, I held these over a heat source until the plastic just started to soften. Then I bent the stems of the leaves down for the bottom-of-the-stack cluster and up for the cluster for the top of the stack. This allowed me to spread the fronds better. The

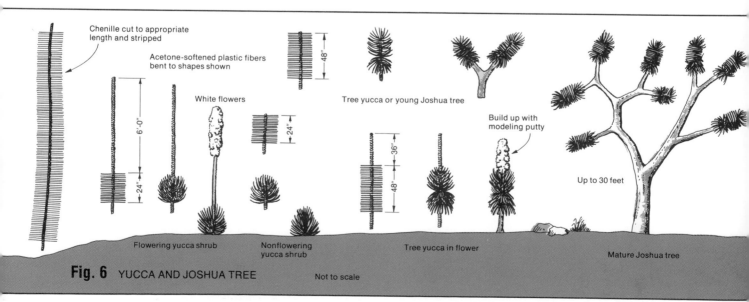

Chenille cut to appropriate length and stripped

Acetone-softened plastic fibers bent to shapes shown

White flowers

48"

6'-0"

24"

24"

Tree yucca or young Joshua tree

36"

48"

Build up with modeling putty

Up to 30 feet

Flowering yucca shrub   Nonflowering yucca shrub   Tree yucca in flower   Mature Joshua tree

Fig. 6 YUCCA AND JOSHUA TREE   Not to scale

Colorado Plateau: red sandstone cliffs with sagebrush and flowering yucca

bottom cluster can be painted Depot Olive; better yet, paint it straw-yellow.

Palms often grow along geological faults, in canyons, or in oases where there is water seepage. In fact, here is your excuse to model water on your desert layout!

CHOLLA

Cholla cacti (fig. 8) can be easily made from juniper or cypress twigs painted light green (Depot Olive lightened with white). Flowers go on the tips of the branches. Use some Woodland Scenics yellow flowers glued with matte medium.

AGAVE

Agave, or century plants (fig. 9), are made from the needle clusters from a plastic pine branch. Airbrush them with Floquil Depot Olive. The stalk, 30 feet high, is made from a twig. Choose one that has one main stem with branches coming off in all directions all along the main stem. Build up the tips of the branches with matte me-

dium or modeling putty and allow to dry thoroughly. Paint the stalk with Depot Olive. Glue Woodland Scenics yellow flowers to the tops of the branch tips with matte medium. Drill or punch a hole through the middle of the leaf cluster, push the stalk through the hole, and glue.

The plastic pine needles can be used for all scales except N; for this scale, look for other plastic or natural materials, or try making a cluster from wire following the technique used for making ocotillo. Depending on the species of agave, leaf length can vary from 3 to 6 feet.

GRASS

Grass can be made using any of the techniques described in scenery books and articles, so I won't repeat them here. The grass should be quite short and somewhat patchy. In fact, for all but the Chihuahuan desert, grass is not considered a normal desert plant. Think more in terms of shrubs for covering ground.

FINAL THOUGHTS

If making some of the plants makes you impatient, remember that you don't need to make a large number of Joshua trees, saguaros, etc., to achieve the effect you want. Most of your plant life should be shrubs; the larger plants are usually widely separated. One Joshua tree or saguaro per square foot on an HO layout is plenty, unless you're modeling a relatively lush, wet desert. Nice, but unnecessary.

Your backdrops should have mountains painted on them. I neglected to do this for the photos, as I was more interested in clearly showing the plants. For a layout, I would definitely have mountains on the backdrop, for no matter where you are in the desert you will always see mountains.

I hope you now have a better understanding of and appreciation for the desert and how to model it. A model desert can be a fascinating and strangely beautiful aspect of your layout. ☼

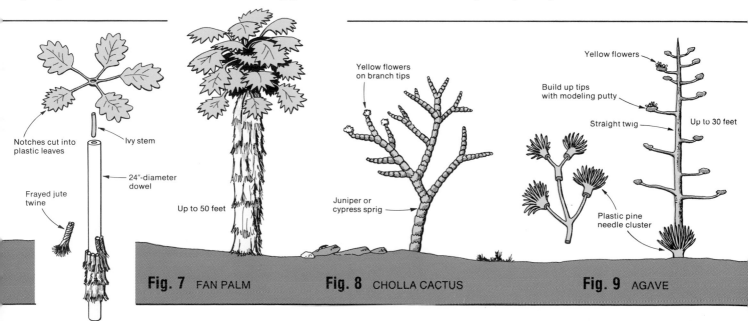

Fig. 7 FAN PALM

Notches cut into plastic leaves

Ivy stem

24"-diameter dowel

Frayed jute twine

Up to 50 feet

Fig. 8 CHOLLA CACTUS

Yellow flowers on branch tips

Juniper or cypress sprig

Fig. 9 AGAVE

Yellow flowers

Build up tips with modeling putty

Straight twig

Up to 30 feet

Plastic pine needle cluster

Fig. 1

Shadow details for background buildings

A clever pencil technique to give added depth to printed cutout structures

BY AL KALBFLEISCH

MOST model railroads require lots of buildings to represent the cities and villages along their routes. The amount of detail in these structures depends upon the proximity of the viewer. Three dimensional details are important when viewers are close to them, but the dimensional relief of these parts becomes almost imperceptible at distances greater than 6 feet. At this range, nearly any building looks good to the viewer if it has a realistic shape, appropriate color, and some well-defined shadows.

Dover Publications Inc., 180 Varick St., New York, NY 10014, publishes a whole series of HO scale paper buildings in book form. The current sets, shown in fig. 1, include an early New England village, a Western frontier town, and Victorian houses. All of the structures used in this project are taken from the Western frontier town set. These buildings are precisely laid out, well-shaped, and appropriately colored; however, they are entirely without shadows or fine details.

As I worked on my town, I found a lot of useful modeling techniques in the Kalmbach softcover book *How to Build Dioramas* by Shepard Paine. The idea of treating the whole town as a diorama came from this book.

My first step in constructing these buildings is made while they are in the flat printed sheet form. By removing a little color here and there and adding some penciled-in details, the buildings take on a whole new — and improved — look.

The trick to adding shadows to a structure of this type depends upon how well you can visualize where shadows fall. Shep Paine suggests we think of the model as being under a large diffused light source. With this in mind, I was able to study the buildings and visualize how the light would affect the various printed textures and details. Any projection from the flat plane of the structure's walls will produce a shadow.

Adding shadows and other details is not very difficult and the process re-

quires few tools. I use a typing eraser which has an abrasive in the rubber, a draftsman's eraser shield, a set of colored pencils, and black lead pencils in several different grades of hardness.

For those who are unfamiliar with it, a draftsman's eraser shield is a thin stainless-steel rectangle with various sizes and shapes of holes punched in it. By placing the shield over the drawing, it is possible to do precision erasing of specific areas.

I do the shadow work on the structures while they are still in the uncut page form. They are easier to handle as full pages and less likely to rip or crease if I get too enthusiastic. I divide my shadowing procedure into two separate steps: removal and addition.

REMOVAL OF COLOR

I use the removal technique to fade the paint in the clapboard siding. The comparison in fig. 2 shows the difference. To do this I use the eraser shield to define the area I'm working on, and then I lightly erase horizontal strips across random boards. In this way I can control how much I lighten any specific board. A light erasing takes only a little ink off, while continued erasing removes more and more color. While I'm on this step I also erase in a few vertical lines to represent water runoff areas.

All windows have light reflections in them, so I modify mine to include these highlights. If you have problems remembering how windows really look, take a look at a nearby building with windows and notice how they reflect their surroundings. Depending upon how you position the eraser shield, it is possible to lighten the upper portions of the windows and reproduce any kind of reflection you feel is appropriate.

I repeat the technique on the roof, as it is the most exposed area of any building, and more signs of weathering should ap-

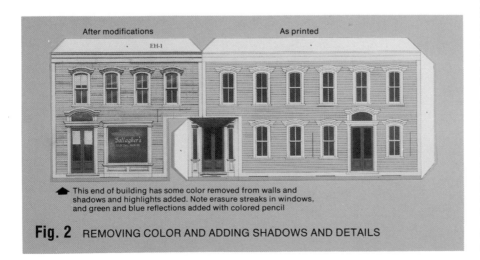

After modifications   As printed

EH-1

This end of building has some color removed from walls and shadows and highlights added. Note erasure streaks in windows, and green and blue reflections added with colored pencil

Fig. 2 REMOVING COLOR AND ADDING SHADOWS AND DETAILS

pear there. Once again I use the erasing process and then remove light streaks in a vertical direction to simulate markings from water runoff.

ADDING SHADOWS AND DETAILS

I use a combination of hard and soft lead pencils to add the shadows, while the colored pencils come in handy for detail items. For heavy shadows I take a soft-lead pencil and make the line under the board wider and darker. See fig. 2. Sometimes this takes several passes to look right, especially under ledges and trim boards. If I want a lighter shadow that is more on the grayish side, I use a harder grade of pencil.

When clapboard siding weathers, the boards have a tendency to warp into an outward curve that pulls the bottom edge away from the wall. In fig. 3 the bottom edges of the siding boards still line up when they are viewed from a point perpendicular to the wall. However, the warped board casts a shadow that gradually increases in width under the outward bend.

I simulate the warped siding by adding a wide dark shadow at the end of a board and then tapering it down to the appropriate-width shadow near the middle of the board. Of course, all of these warps are different, but this makes for an interesting shadow pattern. By tapering the different shadows in both directions, I can easily simulate this warped-board effect.

The colored pencils come in handy to change the hue of light-colored items, such as the building trim boards. I use them to darken a few sheathing boards or individual bricks to get more realistic variety. Just remember to keep these variations subtle so the buildings do not acquire a checkerboard look in the process. Combinations of the colored- and black-lead pencils are perfect for adding board ends, and small dots do a good job of simulating nailheads.

THREE-DIMENSIONAL DETAILS

I followed the Dover Publications general instructions for the assembly of the buildings. However, I did reinforce each structure with heavy illustration board and stripwood as shown in fig. 4. The result is a sturdy group of buildings that should last for many years.

When I finally assemble the reworked buildings, I add some three-dimensional items to make them look right. Figure 5 shows some of these additions, including strips of wood around the foundation (to make an even joint between the building and the scenery), molded plastic steps, stair railings, porch railings, chimneys, and wood balconies.

This mixture of flat shadow detailing and three-dimensional parts combines to create an image of great detail in the viewer's mind. The effect is just like theater scenery — at the audience's viewing distance, it looks great because the viewer's imagination supplies whatever is missing. All the modeler has to do is supply enough visual cues to get the visitor's imagination started. ✿

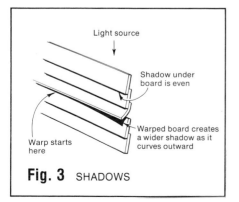

Fig. 3 SHADOWS

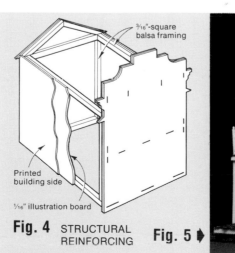

Fig. 4 STRUCTURAL REINFORCING **Fig. 5** ▶

Stafford Swain photos

Modeling with photo prints

BY STAFFORD SWAIN AND JOHN NEHRICH

These three photos illustrate the process of elimination the author used in choosing just the right building for the scene. **Above.** The warehouse looked good, but the spectacular multicolored sign was partially hidden by the brewery, and so he decided to save that one for a better location. **Above right.** The past vintage hotels were interesting, but they towered over the brewery offices, and the late-model cars parked in front were of a different era. **Bottom right.** The Manitoba Bridge building was the right size, but its color was the same as the brewery and coal yard office.

ft. We're looking down McCreary Ave. in Fort Garry on the author's HO scale Canadian National Whiteshell Subdivision layout. The buildings at the end of the street are neither painted nor modeled; they're on a photograph pasted to the backdrop. **Above.** The same scene from above. Note the short distance between tracks and backdrop. The street has also been tapered slightly to force the perspective.

Stafford Swain lists advantages and helpful hints

THE BASIC CONCEPT is simplicity itself: just paste photographs of urban scenes onto your backdrop. That's all there is to it.

Well, not quite. There are a few little wrinkles to deal with. I'm going to try to identify some of them for you and propose a few solutions. I've also identified a few opportunities that may not be immediately obvious to you and list a number of advantages of the technique. And, for good measure, I'll offer a few ideas that haven't been tested yet just in case you wish to run with them.

CONCEPTS AND ADVANTAGES

Some specific advantages come to mind immediately. I'm sure there are others.

● Plain and simple, a color photo is going to be a more complete and accurate rendering of a man-made object (such as a structure) than anything most of us could possibly generate.

● Even if we are endowed with great artistic skills, it isn't easy reaching across a chunk of benchwork to paint with the precision that a well-rendered structure requires. Almost all of the work with photo backdrops can be done at the workbench.

● The "modeling" of favorite buildings, say one with a particularly interesting sign, can be achieved with ease by careful placement of a photo of the building. All of the detail of the building will be there and in living color too. Of course, the right weathering will come along with it.

● A large industrial complex that would overpower the layout (and maybe the modeler) as a complete model can be represented by means of an enlarged photo.

● With some care, your layout's interchange with another modeler's layout could be modeled with common buildings. John Morris, my Canadian Pacific modeling friend, and I are working on this idea, and if it goes together the way we hope, we'll show you in a future issue.

● And finally, there is the obvious opportunity for modelers to share their favorite photos.

PHOTOGRAPHIC CONSIDERATIONS

Probably the most difficult problem to overcome in the initial stages is the simple lack of the appropriate photos to work with. This will take time to overcome, but with a little fieldwork with the trusty 35-mm camera you can do it. Furthermore, if you have modeling friends with similar interests, this can easily become a team project.

What follows are some hints that will be helpful for you to know before you head out with your camera.

● From the standpoint of expense, I recommend slide film. I find that I shoot a lot more pictures than I can really use, and there are usually more than a few that are just plain unusable.

● It can be difficult to get unobstructed photos of buildings in urban areas. Try to get out during times when there are fewer people and vehicles to filter out.

● I find that the early spring and the late fall are the best times to be out because there is no foliage to get in the way. A little amateur retouching will usually hide the odd bare branch that gets in the way.

● Pay attention to the shadows on the buildings. If you need to have the shadows on the opposite side of the building to work it into the backdrop properly, try to get back later (or go earlier in the day) to take the shot. You probably could work in shadows with overpainting if you had to, but the idea here is to minimize your work not add to it.

● Within reason try to get as far back from the subject as you can. For example, with a normal lens on your camera try to stand at the same distance as the viewer would be viewing (in scale) the photo on the layout. This has the effect of minimizing the distortion that will inevitably occur. Needless to say, if extreme it pretty well ends your chances of using the photo.

● For large buildings or industrial complexes it's feasible to capture the entire complex using several shots.

● Modelers of early eras will have to be careful to shoot only buildings that look plausible for their selected time frame.

For anyone who has visited Winnipeg, this "suburbia" scene rings true — houses on the edge of the prairie and a flat horizon. To create the scene the author used six street-corner photos. Note the use of trees (indefinite scale) to disguise the transition between suburbia and the coal yard at left.

Contemporary modelers can just charge right ahead.

• If you want to do a collage of several buildings, similar to my suburbia backdrop (bottom of page 85), it's important to try to stand at uniform distances from the several subjects that you plan to work together. To get the suburbia photos I just stood on the same spot on a number of street corners in an older section of town. Thus all the photos wound up at about the same distance and angle.

PREPARATION AND INSTALLATION

Preparation and installation of the photos isn't particularly difficult, but there are a few tricks that work (and also a few that don't).

To date I've just used basic drugstore prints, and I haven't tried to tailor enlargement sizes, though you could take this approach without too much difficulty (other than additional expense). Another idea that's worth exploring is the use of color photo copying. It certainly is cheaper and may work out very well.

After the selected photos have been printed to an appropriate size, the next step is to cut the building out of the photo. This should be done with a modeler's knife and a straightedge rather than with a scissors.

I usually prefer to mount the photo(s) onto a card backing using rubber cement. Without this card backing I've found that the photos will often curl away from the backdrop with humidity changes. This card backing is particularly useful if you're tieing together several photos into an overall building. It also has the advantage of giving you a free-standing unit to work with. The card backing should also be cut to conform to the outline of the building.

The raw edges should be touched up with paint or a felt-tip pen. And while you're at it, if you're working with several photos (such as I was in my suburbia collage) or if there are details to re-touch/overpaint, you can do this with artist's acrylic paints. Because photographic prints are glossy, as are acrylic paints to a degree, a spray coat of flat varnish is a must at this point.

The photo(s) or collage, as the case may be, can now be mounted on the previously completed backdrop. If you need additional distant backdrop shrubs and trees, you can add these to better work in the photo. Owing to the potential of expansion and contraction, I try to avoid gluing the photo to the backdrop. Instead, I use several track spikes to pin the photo to the backdrop. These can be disguised with a bit of paint if you can't get a bush to sprout in front of them. Another advantage of this mounting method is that any out-of-plumb problems can be readily corrected by yanking a spike or two to straighten things out.

Transitions between three-dimensional models near the backdrop can be tricky, but I've found that nonspecific-sized items, like fences or overhanging trees, will get you out of most problems.

Photographic prints can also be used in other projects where you are willing to settle for only two dimensions, as John will explain next. — *Stafford Swain*

Photos by John Nehrich

We're looking up Broad St. in South Chateaugay on the Rensselaer Polytechnic Institute's HO scale New England, Berkshire & Western layout. The author has used color prints in a different way here, cutting them apart and reassembling them as the two-sided cathedral at the end of the street.

John Nehrich suggests other uses for prints

THERE may be situations where you don't need to model an entire structure — a spot where space is limited, maybe, or where a building meets the backdrop at an angle. Color photographic prints have applications here as well. Let me give you some examples.

ST. JOHN'S CHURCH — A QUASI 3-D BUILDING

One section of Chateaugay on the Rensselaer Polytechnic Institute's New England, Berkshire & Western layout is based on a scene in Plattsburgh, N. Y., looking up Broad Street. The Gothic steeple of St. John's Roman Catholic Church rises prominently above the other buildings. This was a little too far from the backdrop to allow a two-dimensional photo to work, since you could see around it. At the same time, it was also too far from the layout's edge for me to want to model it with a lot of work. First I tried using one print, but that didn't work. Eventually I had two more identical 5 x 7" prints made from the same slide and used them to make a quasi three-dimensional building.

I had originally intended to take photos of both sides of the cathedral, but since one side was blocked by other buildings, I had to settle for a photo of only one side. When the slide came back from Kodak, I pried open the slide mount and flipped the piece of film so the resulting print would be a mirror-image. (Specifying that you want a *backwards* print only confuses the film processors.)

When the prints were returned I cut the image out of each print, then used an ordinary pencil to trace the outline of the cathedral onto .010" brass. I then used tin snips to cut the brass, staying on the inside of the line. Lots of Walthers Goo, with ACC flowed in along the edges, seems to have made the lamination permanent.

I cut off the corner buttress on the near side of each side steeple print. The corner buttress cut from one side was used on the other, at a right angle at the back. Each print contained a two-window segment of the church itself. One segment is still attached to the first print; the other two segments on top of that allowed me to make a four-window-long church, long enough to run back into an obscuring thicket of trees.

Later, I painted out the repeating utility pole that runs up through the roof twice, and I touched up the raw white cut edges with a pencil, followed by a spray of Dullcote.

The backdrop was made from a collage of four prints (two on each side of the street) and an additional one for the free-standing white house on the left — a total of eight prints from six slides.

UNIVERSAL NEWS

This structure was built for the rear of Chateaugay, far from the viewing public. One of the "have-to-model" features was the large sign painted on the side of the building. I decided to use a photographic print of the actual sign as the easiest way to miniaturize this. It would have been very time-consuming to letter this by hand or with decals, difficult to capture the faded character exactly, and nearly impossible to paint the handheld Coke bottle. The real sign is painted

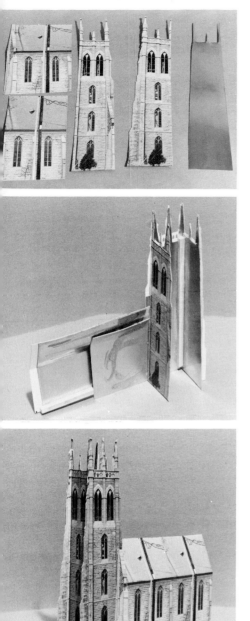

Another use for photographic prints is as a source of signs for industries and businesses. The Universal News signs on this building came from photos, as did the signs in the store windows.

The state highway at Regis makes a sharp bend at the backdrop. To make the turn less noticeable, the author cemented a photo of a farmhouse to the backdrop and strategically placed a few trees.

he author could get to only one side of the cathedral ▸ photograph it, so he had the processor flop the ▸lide and print it backwards. **Top to bottom.** First he ut the building out of the prints; then he cemented the ▸ieces to thin sheet brass; and finally, he reassembled ▸e pieces to make it look like a four-sided structure.

directly on the bare brick — using a print as an overlay seemed to me to be the least objectionable compromise.

The sign is also not as large as on the real building. I have standard-sized prints (3 x 5, 5 x 7, or 8 x 10) made from my slides. In this case, the 3 x 5 version was close enough, while the 5 x 7 print yielded the sign on front. If I wanted the size to be more accurately sized, I would photograph the sign from various distances to end up with one closer to the scale size I'd need. Of course, it is also possible to have custom-sized enlargements made.

When the building was finished, I was faced with the tedious prospect of filling the storefronts. In the store next door I used curtains (cut from a department store catalog) across the whole front, as is often done in a restaurant. The awning was cut from another print.

Front windows in a news store are typically covered with advertisements for cigarettes and other sundry products. Having not thought of this on our last visit to Plattsburgh, N. Y. (the site of the prototype), I found a store in nearby Troy to photograph for this purpose. I cut out the best sections to put in the show windows, being careful to avoid unmistakable references to the present that would be inappropriate to a 1950s pike.

STATE HIGHWAY, REGIS, NY

After crossing over the NEB&W tracks, the state highway heads directly at the backdrop, swerving only at the last moment. I softened the effect by gluing a print of a house onto the backdrop and then surrounding it with flat trees. A permanently placed truck just coming around the bend contributes to the feeling that this road is a through route, rather than a dead end.

Obviously, some artistic ability is helpful in creating the right backdrop for a scene, but here's a technique that will give most of us a shot at getting it right the first time. —*John Nehrich*

Building flats as background structures

BY DAVID W. MESSER
PHOTOS BY BILL MISCHLER

ONE of the real giveaways when it comes to realism in model railroading is the point where layout scenery abruptly ends and backdrop abruptly begins. I have a few suggestions concerning structures that I think might be helpful.

It seems to me that background structures used effectively can help ease this difficult transition in three ways: they can provide an interesting visual transition (or "distraction" if you will) between foreground and backdrop, increasing the apparent depth of the scene; they can suggest a much larger area than is actually modeled (an industrial complex or row of businesses, for example); and finally, they can add industries for increased operation in a limited space.

Background structures can range from full depth (foreground) to flat (background). Depending on their location and viewing angle, they can have from one to three sides unfinished. This is a real time-saver when you have a long background area that you want covered.

Another advantage of background structures is that they can be less detailed than those in the foreground, again saving time. In fact, really all that is needed when a structure is some distance from the viewer is a *suggestion* of detail.

TECHNIQUES

The ideas below represent a few of the techniques and principles I have learned in building background structures.

• Before starting an area, consider the overall scene — size, viewing angle, height, relationship to adjacent areas — in terms of the effect you are trying to create.

• Avoid single large structures; instead, group several small- to moderate-size buildings in logical clusters. This has the effect of suggesting more units than there really are — a form of selective compression. The most pleasing arrangement can often be arrived at by the use of "dummy" buildings of cardboard with windows and doors drawn in. Try several arrangements until you find the one that looks best.

• Provide a transition of structure depth and detail from front to back. This increases the apparent depth of the scene. Using one building to hide a portion of another also enhances this illusion, particularly if the scene shifts as the viewer changes location. Other techniques related include visual elements on otherwise flat units such as loading platforms, signs, lights — even vines — and associated details such as vehicles, figures, utility components, or debris.

• For variety use a mix of kits, kitbashed structures, and scratchbuilt units. Sometimes just a different color scheme, leaving off or adding parts, and combining components from different kits changes their appearance completely and avoids the "just-like-everyone-else's" look.

• Wherever possible — and this certainly isn't limited to background units — model *real* buildings. Look around, shoot pictures, and take notes about prototype structures that will fit the scene you have in mind (either as is or scaled down), and use selective compression to capture the essence of a building.

• Include buildings with fronts facing away from the viewer. This has the dual advantage of displaying the seldom-modeled but often more interesting back (track side) and, if it is a kit structure, of being able to use the front on another unit somewhere else.

• Consider partial structures angled to the backdrop. These are particularly effective with a siding track running alongside, even if there's room for only one car. Integration of structures into the railroad scheme adds interest, realism, and increased operating possibilities.

• For adjacent groups of structures, use modular bases separate from the layout for ease of construction and installation. Row houses can use common structural elements running the length of several units.

ILLUMINATION

Contrary to popular belief, flat or nearly flat structures can be realistically illuminated both inside and out. Properly done, this enhances the illusion of depth and can be quite striking, especially in a city or industrial grouping. The secret is to pay close attention to a few general principles for lighting structures, using a slightly lower level of illumination for flat structures than for full-depth units.

• Use a light intensity appropriate to the type and area of the structure. For instance, a retail store in an apartment building would most likely be brighter than the apartments above.

• Block off some windows completely and vary the intensity in others, giving the effect of a building with depth and increasing the apparent size.

• Use grain-of-wheat and/or miniature bulbs in series (to reduce intensity, increase bulb life, and minimize heat buildup). Colored bulbs, where appropriate, also add interest.

• Position bulbs to avoid "hot spots." Use a medium-gray color for the inside back wall. All other surfaces should be white for even light distribution in a given area.

• Avoid light leaks. Seal all window and corner joints, and make sure walls (particularly the front) are opaque. Even colored plastic may require a coat of dark paint on the inside walls.

• All wiring should be positioned out of sight, preferably on the back of the wall facing the viewer. Use of common, or bus, wiring in groups of units (with one pair of leads extending through the benchwork) greatly simplifies the under-the-table wiring.

INTERIOR DETAIL

A background structure need not have extensive interior detail to look realistic. Depending on location, sometimes a very few items visible from the normal viewing angle will suffice to suggest more. Use of frosted window material, awnings, and shades all enhance realism while reducing or even eliminating the need for interior detailing. Even plain acetate picks up some light and screens out a clear view.

The photos accompanying this article illustrate many of the principles outlined above. The important thing to realize is that structures not only have a place as part of the background of a layout, but they can also improve overall realism, increase operating possibilities, and add greatly to your enjoyment of the layout. ⚙

Above: Dummy cardboard buildings work very well for giving an idea of what the final scene will look like. Here three layers of structures in only 2 feet give the impression of greater depth. Left: This photo illustrates the use of building fronts. Three are Magnuson models; the third from the left is from two Lytler & Lytler kits. Below: This backside shot shows where the other parts of kits have gone. All of these represent leftovers from other kits. Remember, railroads *often* come in at the back door.

e two views above illustrate a couple of principles about using structures backgrounds. The buildings at right in the top photo are scratchbuilt, ng commercial castings and only a little detail since these will be partially hidden. The rear view illustrates how common structural members reinforce each other. Note also the blocking out of window groupings and sealant around windows to prevent light leaks. Note varying light intensity in the scene below.

The urban scenery of Severna Park

A downtown industrial district with tracks in the streets can be one of the most interesting scenes on a model railroad

BY PAUL J. DOLKOS

SCENERY. That usually connotes mountains, a seacoast, or perhaps a city skyline. It certainly doesn't bring to mind a downtown industrial district with loft buildings, warehouses, manufacturing plants, and tracks in the streets. Such a district is not what you find in travel brochures, or even where railfans go trooping off to with their cameras for the definitive action shot.

But for the model railroader, the downtown industrial district with tracks in the street may be some of the best scenery ever. At Maryland's Severna Park Model Railroad Club, where fine scenery is the norm [June 1973 MR], its city scenery overshadows the

mountains in the opinion of many. Interestingly, what has become a highlight on the club's HO scale Chesapeake & Allegheny RR. really started out as a solution to a scenery problem.

As the main line loops around the layout room it passes underneath the passenger station and freight yards by about 18″. Letting the lower track just dive into a hillside through a tunnel did not seem to the clubmembers to be very interesting or appropriate, with a major passenger terminal sitting inches away. There was an area of only 4 square feet to work with.

Inspiration was only 20 miles down the road, along the wharves and adja-

cent industrial-commercial-residential district around Baltimore's Fells Point. Starting with some wheat and flour shipments in the middle 1700's, this area has had a couple of hundred years to develop character. Structures here range from federal-style loft buildings, to victorian storefronts, to World War I brick and cement warehouses and factories. There were and are a variety of enterprises, including lumber wholesalers, coal dealers, fertilizer plants, and grain storage depots.

The railroads came to Baltimore's portside in the 1830's, so many of the buildings were already in place. It took every trick in the book to snake the

Maryland's Severna Park Model Railroad Club has captured the spirit of the Baltimore waterfront area through selective compression. This scene recognizable on a visit to the prototype, although on the layout the Rukert Terminals Co. building is scaled down and the pierhouse is shortened. ↑The Nagel Steel Tank Corp. is an example of a heavy-industry model in a small area. Its placement allows it size without being overpowering.

Chesapeake Lines Warehouse No. 3 is built of scored and aged balsa. At the prototype site this weathered building is a PC freight house.

An overhead crane loads one of the products of the Nagel Steel Tank Corp. The crane is made of styrene, as is the abandoned wooden shed.

track down the streets and the spurs into and beside the buildings. Sharp curves and special trackwork were mandatory. This dictated the use of small locomotives such as 0-4-0's. The most famous switching power was the Baltimore & Ohio's "Little Joe" dockside. Today both the B&O and Penn Central use rubber-tired tractors or tugs fitted with railroad couplers for switching.

It didn't take much poking around the area by the club's structure and scenery builder, Logan Holtgrewe, and President Sam Shepherd to realize that such a switching district would fit nicely into the 4-square-foot area they needed to fill. They felt it would be easy to make the 18″ vertical separation with tall buildings. No space would have to

be given up for a normal slope of a hillside or mountain. The mainline track could convincingly disappear behind a building. And they could add some interesting switching possibilities with several spurs. This is usually tough to do in a square area, unless you do what the prototype does on the Baltimore waterfront.

Holtgrewe and Shepherd began the model of the area called East Baltimore on the club railroad by closely following the actual track layout at one street intersection. Code 70 rail was spiked directly to a Homasote base. True to the prototype, Shepherd built many of the turnouts with single points. Holtgrewe began building structures by reproducing a block of buildings located at the prototype site, using Holgate & Reyn-

olds plastic brick and block materials. A few changes were made in door and window layout, and the model block reflects somewhat more prosperous times. A few of the other structures at the prototype scene were also small enough to be reproduced faithfully.

At this point, free-lancing in structure design began in earnest, for even the relatively compact major structures at the scene are too big to be duplicated foot for foot. The Rukert Terminals wharf structure is a consolidation, with the brick warehouse portion simplified and the pierhouse shortened. What is the present Penn Central President Street Freight Station in the prototype scene is represented in the model as the Chesapeake Lines Warehouse No. 3. The warehouse does use the same shape

This block of buildings on Thames St. in Baltimore (top photo) was the inspiration for the Duvall-Nagel block on the club layout. The models, which closely follow the prototype, are constructed of brick materials and styrene.

The use of rubber-tired vehicles to switch railroad cars in Baltimore industrial districts dates back to the 1920's. The Penn Central currently uses these internal-combustion tractors which replaced some battery-powered units.

A variety of tall structures eases the transition from different track levels on the layout. The Bruha Transfer structure, for instance (upper left), is 18" above street level. Residential townhouses are seen in a rear view of the East Baltimore scene (center). The Sanitary Feather Co. structure and sign (above) are based on Chicago prototypes seen in a 1920's photo.

and general design as the PC station.

The rear portion of the model scene required buildings five stories or higher to conceal the change in benchwork height and provide a backdrop for the foreground. In the prototype such structures are several blocks away. The modelbuilders found many suitable designs in brick, block, and stone that would blend nicely with the foreground. They also noted the use of passageways between some industrial buildings to span tracks or streets, as well as concrete highway viaducts. Both of these items were incorporated into the model to help the illusion that the main track disappears behind a building. They serve as effective foils in concealing the point at which the track ducks under the higher benchwork.

The basic shapes of the larger buildings were formed with heavy styrene and covered with plastic brick material. Of special interest are the windows. Achieving uniformity in the 80 or 90 windows a large building might have would be nearly impossible if they were built individually or ruled with ink — to say nothing of the tedium. Holtgrewe devised a jig-stencil so that the muntins could be sprayed on the clear window material. It was a two-step process. The vertical muntins were sprayed-on first. When the paint was dry, a stencil for the horizontal bars was used. The method is fast, and it creates a convincing window even when viewed up close.

Good signs always add a lot to any scene. The ones in the model of East Baltimore were made with dry transfer

alphabets in various sizes and styles, purchased at commercial art supply stores. Some signs are copied directly from the prototype. Others are based on clubmembers' names.

The Friesware billboard (member Frank Fries is with Tupperware) features a coffeepot that is actually half a plastic toy from a child's tea set. The resulting sign is typical of the elaborate advertising done for consumer products in metropolitan areas. The cutout letter signs on the roof of Nagel Steel Tank and Sanitary Feather Co. are just that. Dry transfer letters were rubbed on styrene sheet to provide a pattern. The letters were then cut out, painted as required, and mounted on a wire support framework.

The street surfaces are heavy Strath-

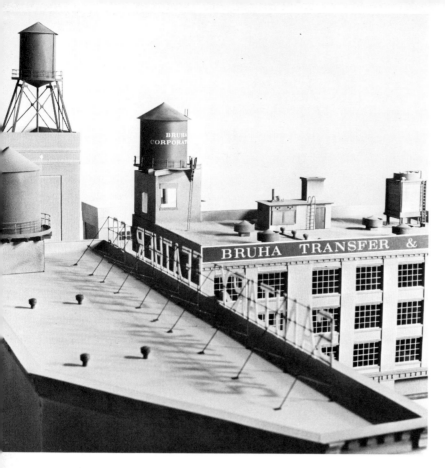

(Above) Water tanks, cooling units, and vents are important details on the roads of scenery builder Logan Holtgrewe's buildings. (Below) Holtgrewe (left) and President Sam Shepherd inspect factory detailing.

(Above right) Here is a look at the backyards of the East Baltimore townhouses shown on page 92. A model backyard wouldn't be complete without the usual screened-in porches, fences, garbage cans, and doghouses.

more board. Plaster and other materials were considered and rejected because of maintenance and durability factors. The cutting and fitting of the board were made simple by dusting the rails with colored plaster that the club normally uses for zip texturing. The Strathmore was sprayed with an adhesive and laid on top of the dusted rails. The powder transferred to the board, creating a perfect pattern. The cutouts were made following the plaster lines. The pieces were pressed into place and can easily be removed for maintenance. The final step was airbrushing the area a street surface color and cleaning the rails.

Once started, it's hard to stop urban sprawl, even on model railroads. Already construction has begun on a city skyline, using building flats that will extend from the club's East Baltimore area along the wall and around the back of the freight yards.

Perhaps, just perhaps, urban scenery is the perfect setting for our model railroads. It is in the cities that the prototype comes to grips with the same relative dimensions that try modelers' souls in basements, attics, or spare bedrooms. Why do we punish ourselves erecting spindly trestles and casting rock tunnels, trying to capture the majesty of mountain railroading in 4x 8 feet? There is a world of prototype railroading where close clearances and tight curves are very real. It translates into model form very nicely.

The art of using mirrors

How to expand your layout in the same space

BY JOHN ALLEN

This scene at Great Divide yard on the Gorre & Daphetid demonstrates one of John Allen's favorite mirror effects: doubling a stub-end yard. The mirror was placed so that viewers ordinarily could not see themselves, but when Jim Findley popped up through the access hatch he gave the trick away.

JOHN ALLEN outlined this article for MODEL RAILROADER *in October of 1970. He had prepared photos and drawings and had completed notes for the text in December 1970, when he wrote to then-editor Linn Westcott that he had just counted over 30 mirrors on his famous Gorre & Daphetid. For some reason — probably projects that interested him more — he did not finish the article before his death in 1973. Kalmbach Books Editor Bob Hayden found John's handwritten notes while completing Linn Westcott's book,* MODEL RAILROADING WITH JOHN ALLEN, *and prepared this article for publication — more than 11 years after it was begun.*

MIRRORS on my Gorre & Daphetid RR. excite or bring favorable comment from more of my visitors than any other feature. My railroad, though large by private layout standards, is much smaller than it appears. Visitors seem to experience a ripple of excitement after they realize that much of the visual illusion of distance on my layout comes from the careful use of mirrors.

I have been using mirrors for over 25 years on both my present and previous GD layouts. Mirrors have a marvelous ability to apparently punch a hole in a wall or open up and enlarge a confined space, and most model railroads are by necessity built in confined spaces. Although you wouldn't think that a way of enlarging your space to apparently twice its size without increasing room size or construction time is something you could afford to disregard lightly, mirrors are used on few model railroads.

Mirrors, of course, aren't the only way to expand space on your layout. Painted backdrops and diorama-like reduced-scale modeling against a wall also help enlarge the visual effect and, to the single-eyed camera, may do the job better than a mirror. But because our two-eyed depth perception can be only slightly fooled, flat and three-dimensional ruses are not nearly as effective as well-placed mirrors.

These views show the mirror at Port Plastics both before and after the buildings and scene were finished. In the finished view notice the car on the track leading into the central building. That's really only half a car on half a track, and what appears to be two fellows talking is actually one figure painted differently front and back.

On the second GD, above, John placed the Teaby Fire Extinguisher Co. against a mirror to double the size of the burned out building. The smoke painted on the mirror both disguised the joint and made the fire seem to be still smoldering. Look closely and you can see where the track butts against the mirror, at a 90 degree angle as shown in fig. 2. In the first of the construction views below, John covered his mirror with wrapping paper. He then removed the paper to show the mirror's dramatic effect.

MIRRORS LARGE AND SMALL

Mirrors can be large or small. My largest — shown above and to the right of the central peak in the photo on page 95 — is 6 feet × 2 feet, my smallest only 2″ × 3″. There are about three dozen mirrors on my railroad, but I doubt if an observant visitor spots more than a third of them. The rest do their job of enlarging or enhancing without being noticed. The locations of the most important ones are shown in fig. 1.

The large mirrors provide the most expansion and also are the easiest to spot. They can be used to expand the whole room or to enlarge just one area such as a yard. Small mirrors can be used to punch holes through a confining wall, and to continue a street or multiply the area inside a miniature building or mine shaft.

Properly placed on a layout, mirrors are difficult to see. If they stand out as being mirrors, you have probably done the job poorly. Mirrors put in without care and study won't be an improvement. As with any other contrived feature, they must be planned for and worked into the layout to

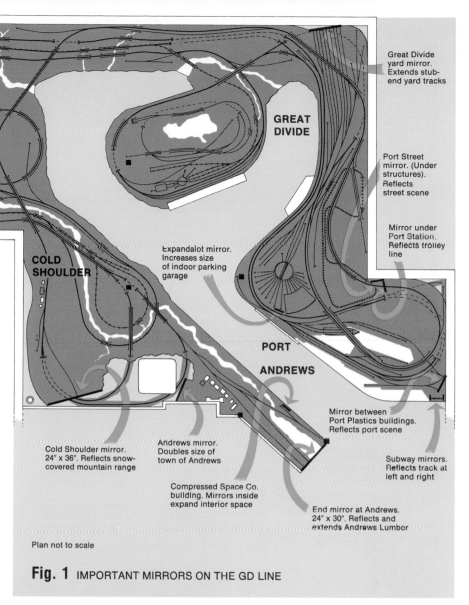

Nika mirror. 24" x 6'-0". Largest on layout. Reflects town of Akin area

Great Divide yard mirror. Extends stub-end yard tracks

GREAT DIVIDE

AKIN

Port Street mirror. (Under structures). Reflects street scene

Mirror under Port Station. Reflects trolley line

COLD SHOULDER

Expandalot mirror. Increases size of indoor parking garage

PORT ANDREWS

Mirror between Port Plastics buildings. Reflects port scene

Cold Shoulder mirror. 24" x 36". Reflects snow-covered mountain range

Andrews mirror. Doubles size of town of Andrews

Subway mirrors. Reflects track at left and right

Compressed Space Co. building. Mirrors inside expand interior space

End mirror at Andrews. 24" x 30". Reflects and extends Andrews Lumber

Plan not to scale

Fig. 1 IMPORTANT MIRRORS ON THE GD LINE

get a good effect. I have developed several rules for placing mirrors on a layout, rules you should remember lest your mirrors double the bad features of your layout instead of enhancing its good ones.

WHAT NOT TO DO — THE DON'TS

Two rules are important when planning mirrors for your layout. First, and foremost, the Great Don't: never ever place a mirror where you will be able to see yourself, other operators, or other full-size, non-model-railroad objects in it. To do so is to destroy the space-expanding feature we are out to achieve.

Second, do not place a mirror where the viewer will be able to see both a moving train and the moving reflection of it at the same time. In other words, do not put a mirror where a track passes nearby in front of it, because if the train can be seen scooting by with its mirror-image reflected, the reflected image is most distracting.

Trees, billboards, building fronts, retaining walls, or a cut might be used to hide either the reflection or the train itself if a track must pass near a mirror. Putting a tunnel in front of the mirror or passing the track behind it will hide both train and re-

flection, and is often useful to disguise the oversupply of track on our layouts.

Most rules have exceptions, and the exception to this one is that the train's reflection is not distracting when stub-end yard tracks approach a mirror at a 90-degree angle. Since all train movement in such a yard will be slow switching, and because the cars will be moving in opposite directions and the engine will be far enough from its reflection to require an eye shift, this is one of the most effective and pleasing of all mirror tricks.

MIRROR QUALITY

The quality of the larger mirrors is important; that of the smaller ones less so. Optical perfection is not required, but both large and small mirrors should be flat, of reasonably good quality,* and not discolored. If the glass has a slight wave, the distortion in the reflection you see as your head moves is distracting and weakens the illusion. Discolored mirrors alter the intensity and color of the reflected image, which detracts from their enlarging effect. Tinted mirrors have little use on a model railroad;

*John bought most of his mirrors from the Edmund Scientific Co.

Some of John's mirrors were just for fun: what he called "the world's largest HO indoor parking lot" actually held just two automobiles, but seemed to stretch to infinity. The cars were painted differently on the sides away from the viewer, who looked into the garage through a one-way mirror.

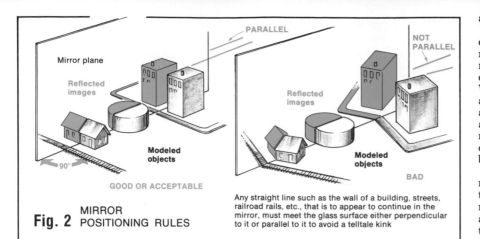

Mirror plane

Reflected images

Modeled objects

90°

PARALLEL

NOT PARALLEL

Reflected images

Modeled objects

BAD

GOOD OR ACCEPTABLE

Fig. 2 MIRROR POSITIONING RULES

Any straight line such as the wall of a building, streets, railroad rails, etc., that is to appear to continue in the mirror, must meet the glass surface either perpendicular to it or parallel to it to avoid a telltale kink

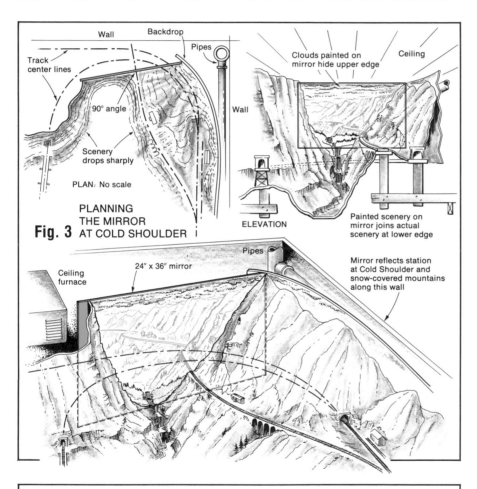

Wall

Backdrop

Pipes

Track center lines

90° angle

Scenery drops sharply

PLAN, No scale

Fig. 3 PLANNING THE MIRROR AT COLD SHOULDER

Clouds painted on mirror hide upper edge

Ceiling

Wall

ELEVATION

Painted scenery on mirror joins actual scenery at lower edge

Ceiling furnace

24" x 36" mirror

Pipes

Mirror reflects station at Cold Shoulder and snow-covered mountains along this wall

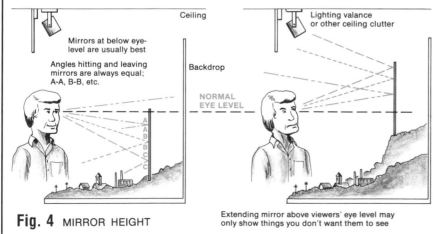

Ceiling

Mirrors at below eye-level are usually best

Angles hitting and leaving mirrors are always equal; A-A, B-B, etc.

Lighting valance or other ceiling clutter

Backdrop

NORMAL EYE LEVEL

Fig. 4 MIRROR HEIGHT

Extending mirror above viewers' eye level may only show things you don't want them to see

at least, I haven't found any use for them.

The thinner the mirror the better, because distortion won't be magnified as much as in a thicker mirror. However, in most cases, the thicker the glass, the less distortion in the surface of the mirror. With large mirrors distortion will be quite apparent, and plate glass mirrors are usually needed. Plate glass mirrors are usually $\frac{3}{16}$" thick or thicker, crystal glass mirrors $\frac{1}{8}$". These thicknesses require extra care to hide the gaps where scenery or buildings touch the glass.

Crystal glass will do for medium-sized mirrors, say 2 feet across or less, provided the distortion in the glass is positioned to run horizontally. That way, as you move around the room the distortion is least noticeable. Have the glass cut to size with this specification. Plate mirrors won't require this, but cost about twice as much.

Avoid lesser quality mirrors than crystal unless they will be very small, 6" or less across. Optical-quality front-surface mirrors are needed only in a few unusual places, such as inside a building or in a confined area that can be examined very closely. Since front-surface mirrors are almost impossible to clean without damaging them, they must be protected from smoke and fingers. See-through mirrors can also be used for special effects, such as my underground parking lot.

RULES FOR POSITIONING MIRRORS

Now we come to rules for placing mirrors on the layout. First, I want to restate and reemphasize the Great Don't: mirrors must be positioned such that only models and model scenery are reflected, not aisleways, other people, and certainly not the viewer himself. This puts a considerable limitation upon mirror placement.

Next, plan each mirror so that strong, low lighting won't strike the mirror. Such lighting will reveal surface dirt, and since any dirt will be shown in duplicate, such lighting will make frequent cleaning of the mirror a necessity. If you must use strong, low lighting, try to provide access and design surrounding details so cleaning is practical. By the way, the resin from cigarette smoke is by far the worst offender in dirtying mirrors.

Since a mirror reflects everything at the same angle, for the best appearance of continuity ground or walls generally look best when coming into contact with the mirror at 90 degree angles. The second most valuable approach of scenery to a mirror is parallel. This doubles the reflected scenery too. See fig. 2.

In most situations scenery and structures adjacent to mirrors should be either parallel or at right angles to the mirror surface, both horizontally and vertically. This rule can sometimes be broken advantageously, but not with track when it comes in contact with the mirror. All track butting against the mirror must be at right angles to it, so that the rail appears to continue into the mirror. See fig. 3.

Every mirror must stand perfectly vertical. Generally it's best to have the ground at a right angle to the mirror where they come in contact; any other angle will cause a sharp break between the real and reflected ground, and the mirror will double the angle. Even if the scenery is the side of a hill or cliff, where it contacts the mirror it should touch at a right angle.

HIDING THE EDGES OF MIRRORS

The edges of each mirror must be logically disguised. This is important. The bottom edge presents little difficulty, because it meets the ground, but the sides must be overlapped all the way to the top edge by modeled objects such as buildings, a cliff in the scenery, or a near-right-angle wall. When a mirror rises all the way to the ceiling, only extraordinarily high buildings and mountain cliffs work well. In fact, where the ceiling is very high above the the layout, a mirror may be so difficult to disguise effectively that you won't be able to use one.

The top edge of the mirror is the most difficult to hide, unless it goes up to touch the ceiling, which usually presents a problem in hiding the sides. Also, any part of a mirror that is above normal eye level has little value, unless there is backdrop or scenery across the room that will be reflected in it. See fig. 4.

If such a mirror reflects ceiling and light fixtures, it violates the Great Don't, which is a distinct disadvantage, especially considering that most of us try to minimize the ceiling and bring the eyes down away from the corners and lights with dropped valances. Using a mirror large enough to reach all the way to the ceiling runs up the cost of the mirror, too.

To get around this, I have used clouds and smoke to hide the top edges of two large mirrors in large open areas on the GD Line, as shown in fig. 5. I've handled small mirrors near buildings with overpasses and high enclosed walkways that span a street to connect one building to another. This method provides a see-through look. If a bridge or viaduct is logical, this too might hide the top. These are effective provided the the top of the overpass or walkway is at eye level or above; if they are below the viewers' horizon line the mirror always looks phony. See fig. 6.

Clouds and smoke aren't as hard to paint as you might think. Remember, anything painted on the mirror glass is doubled, so to blend the edge, use only half the paint that would be required to make an opaque cloud on a window. Like the walkway disguise, the cloud or smoke line should be above the viewer's eye, and similar smoke or clouds should be repeated on the backdrop behind the mirror.

Finally, it is important that any sky backdrop mirrored from across the room duplicate the color and light intensity of the sky surrounding or adjacent to the mirror. The angle of light striking structures and clouds in the reflected image should also be the same as in the adjacent scenery. If smoke trails rising from chimneys are painted on your backdrop, those behind a mirror and those reflected in the mirror should drift the same way.

SOMETHING YOU SHOULD TRY

I doubt if there is any model railroad with one or more edges against a wall that could not incorporate mirrors of various sizes to expand its limited space advantageously. Try it on your layout, being sure to analyze the situation and observe the rules. When the mirror has been installed correctly and scenery or buildings completed nearby, it should not look like a mirror at all, but only a continuation of the area in the modeled scene. ✿

The view of Great Divide while still unfinished shows how the mirror there was placed at the end of the stub yard — there are only two actual passenger cars in the photo. Compare this with the color picture on page 95 and you'll see some of John's techniques for hiding a mirror's edges.

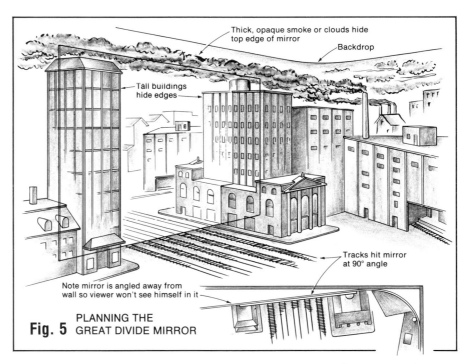

Thick, opaque smoke or clouds hide top edge of mirror

Backdrop

Tall buildings hide edges

Tracks hit mirror at 90° angle

Note mirror is angled away from wall so viewer won't see himself in it

Fig. 5 PLANNING THE GREAT DIVIDE MIRROR

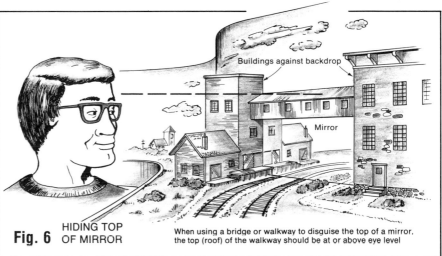

Buildings against backdrop

Mirror

Fig. 6 HIDING TOP OF MIRROR

When using a bridge or walkway to disguise the top of a mirror, the top (roof) of the walkway should be at or above eye level

1   2   3

Build a backdrop collage

How to combine painted backdrop scenery with magazine cutouts and three-dimensional structures

BY EARL SMALLSHAW

THE backdrop collage on my HO layout incorporates flat painted scenery, cutouts, and three-dimensional buildings. It dresses up my pike in a way that I feel is very realistic and somewhat unusual.

I started by painting the background. I used acrylics: gray for distant hills and a mixture of various greens in the foreground hills. The church steeple, fig. 1, is the only detail painted directly on the backdrop.

Next I applied the first cutout: fig. 2. These buildings were drawn on cardstock and colored with Floquil paints. The bottom area of this cutout was airbrushed with white to create separation and distance between this cutout and the next one to be applied. The second cutout was applied over the first. This cutout, fig. 3, is really two pieces—the buildings and a grassy hillside hiding the lower portions of the buildings.

The cutouts were then bracketed by three-dimensional buildings: fig. 4. The three buildings on the left are only building fronts. See fig. 5. The bar was

covered with brick paper. Signs in the window are from a Fine Scale Miniatures sign sheet. All other lettering was hand-painted.

The hotel was sheathed with clapboards of cardstock. SS Ltd. windows were used. The hotel, once quite fashionable, has been reduced to a 50-cents-per-night flophouse. The cannery next door probably led to its downfall.

Clerke's Cannery is a brownstone building with bricks scribed in it with a modeler's knife. Three of the finials removed from SS Ltd. windows in the main structure were used here to decorate the roofline of this building. The lower half of the hotel and cannery were not modeled, since they were to be hidden later by a foreground structure. The main plant of the Middletown Container Co. is about 2" deep and extends to 7" deep beyond the opening in the backdrop.

The original Middletown Container Co. factory, a frame structure seen in fig. 6, was positioned next. It was sheathed with clapboards made from

IBM cardstock, individually applied, to create a natural aged appearance. The foundation, as with the main structure, is stone, and is made in the same manner. The shingles are made of latex rubber. I made a plaster mold of a commercial shingle sheet and painted liquid latex rubber over the mold. The result: an image of the original shingle sheet in rubber—sort of like the rubber mold scenery technique in reverse. Why go through this process when I just duplicate what I had in the first place? Well, obviously, I can now duplicate shingle material for other structures inexpensively. But more important, it was an experiment to see if it could be done, so that I might use this technique in other areas of construction at other times.

Once the shingle material was applied, I airbrushed it grimy black and weathered it with grime. A hand-painted sign, barely visible on the side of the structure, was painted directly over the clapboards and three boarded-up windows. This facility is now used only for

7   8   9

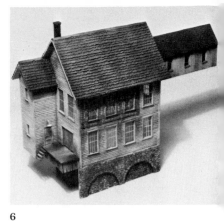

5

6

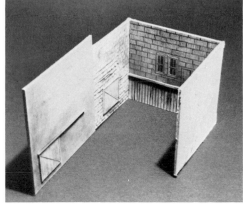

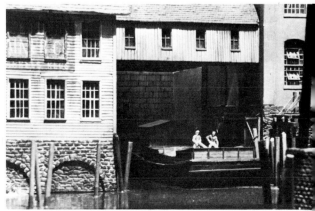

10

11

12

13

14

local deliveries and receiving. Notice how the top edge of the opening in the backdrop was hidden by the connecting ramp between the old and new parts of the factory complex. See fig. 7.

The main structure, fig. 8, is a typical turn-of-the-century factory, with a mansard roof, stone foundation, and freight doors for both barge and rail traffic. The foundation was laminated with 1/32″ balsa sheet. The "stone" was burned in with a child's woodburning tool. Tempera colors of brown, black, and white were used to paint the foundation. The walls were covered with brick paper and painted with a dull brick wash to tone down the garish color of the brick paper. The sign, "Mid-

dletown Container Co.," was made with dry transfers on a black panel. The windows in the roof, from SS Ltd., were altered slightly—the finials were cut off—to make them less ornate. The roof was shingled with diamond-shaped "shingles" made of construction paper cut with pinking shears. An SS Ltd. billboard was added to help disguise the narrow roofline.

The extension of the main structure, fig. 9, has brick walls and a stone foundation, applied in the same manner as on the main building. A portion of the foundation was left unfinished because it was to be covered with scenery later. The roof was covered with Campbell shingle strips. The lettering on the walls

is dry transfers. After application, the lettering was scratched with a modeler's knife to remove parts of the letters, simulating years of exposure. This structure is deeper than the main building, to match the backdrop as it curves away from the foreground: fig. 10.

The building fronts in fig. 11 were positioned behind the backdrop to continue the scene from the foreground structures through the opening in the backdrop. See fig. 12. All detail was drawn on with pen and ink, and no attempt for fine detail was made here.

A trestle, seen in fig. 13, was added next to service the main structure. The trestle snakes its way between the building walls and the bridge supports before it is able to parallel the factory. Here, the finished products are shipped by rail to distant customers.

More cutouts I prepared for the backdrop are shown in fig. 14. This group of houses was clipped from *Yankee* magazine. (Many magazines are excellent sources, particularly *National Geographic*.) The coloring was further emphasized by touching up with acrylics to highlight the sunlit portions of the buildings. The background foliage was colored to match that of the backdrop. This did not require any particular art talent. It was almost like painting a coloring book, except smaller brushes were used. Below the group of houses in the picture is another cutout of a house and shed with a connecting line of washing. This is as it was clipped from the magazine. Depending on the coloring of the magazine scene, I found some touchup was almost always required. I used care to select scenes that were at the correct perspective and appropriate size for the backdrop requirements.

Fig. 15 shows the area of the backdrop (directly above the roof in the center) before the cutout in fig. 14 was positioned. The "after" picture, fig. 16, shows the cutout positioned and glued in place, blending with the painted hills of the backdrop. Even close examination can't expose this "hand-painted" backdrop as a magazine cutout.

15

16

Creating your own backdrop

How to build and paint a realistic backdrop for your model railroad

BY ROBERT HAMM
PHOTOS BY THE AUTHOR

A PAINTED BACKDROP is an effective addition to the scenery of a model railroad. It fosters the illusion that the mountains and valleys extend far beyond their three-dimensional borderlines. Many of us never try painting our own backdrop because we consider the project beyond our ability or just too much effort. Often it is overlooked until the layout is too far along.

Having long admired the backdrop efforts of John Allen, Francis Lee Jacque [May 1962 MR, out of print], and other model railroaders, I resolved to paint one for my Colorado narrow gauge layout. The layout has been under construction for several years now. Along with building the benchwork, handlaying the track, kitbuilding a number of cars and structures, I've painted about 40 percent of a planned 36-foot backdrop of Colorado mountain scenes. So far I'm pleased with the results, and I've concluded that it isn't so difficult after all. As you read on I'll try to describe the approach and techniques that evolved from those efforts.

The project is divided into five phases: planning, construction, selecting the scene, premixing paints, and painting the backdrop.

PLANNING

A backdrop should be put up and painted as early as possible. Trying to put up wooden supports and attach the backdrop to them across 3 feet of semifinished layout is courting disaster. And attempting to paint the backdrop at that stage of construction is an act of sheer masochism. I planned to finish each backdrop section before I put in scenery, but I wound up with a sore back and near blindness from painting the last section by squirming up between the benchwork joists.

Being able to eliminate corners and hide pipes is one of the benefits of a backdrop. The location of the support columns and the heating system in my basement presented a typical problem in layout planning. They were in the way. My solution was to partition off a furnace room and run a short partition out to the remaining support column.

While this solved one problem and created

A portion of the author's backdrop for his new narrow gauge railroad can be seen in this photo. A painted backdrop creates the illusion that the layout is much larger.

Fig. 1. The author's backdrop is split into two overlapping sections with a space between them. The lighter portion is the landscape and darker is the sky.

some interesting scene separators, I wound up with several new corners: two inside corners, one outside corner, and the end of the partition hiding the lone support column. The backdrop provided an uninterrupted curve around the corners. I used a 2-foot-radius backdrop curve to round the 90 degree corners. The end of the double-sided partition was concealed with a teardrop shaped curve in the backdrop. A radius of about a foot seemed to produce a large enough curvature. None of the curved corners, including the latter, covered up much usable layout surface. I suggest, however, that you consider space for the backdrop in your planning.

In planning the backdrop height it's important to understand and establish a horizon. By definition the horizon is a line where, in the absence of mountains, the sky meets the land or sea. To put it another way, it is the lowest level at which you can see sky. Mountains and other structures can extend above the horizon. As you gaze out over the landscape the horizon always appears at eye level. Likewise, the horizon on your backdrop should be at eye level. Since my eye level is about 66″, I established the horizon there. This is the only way to get the right perspective with regard to your three-dimensional scenery.

Lighting is a related area requiring planning consideration. The type of lights and their placement will determine how the backdrop looks. For example, a backdrop painted under incandescent lights will probably look too blue under fluorescent lights. Strong directional light will cast shadows from buildings. If you intend to use directional lighting you should make sure your painted shadows are in the same direction as the actual ones. The best solution is to install the lights before you paint. At least use the same type — incandescent or fluorescent — when you paint that you will use to light the layout.

CONSTRUCTION

I physically split my backdrop into two overlapping sections, positioning the lower landscape section about 2½″ in front of the upper sky section. See fig. 1. The slight separation seems to give a three-dimensional effect to the mountains, an effect which I like. But the primary reason for the separation is that I plan to light the space between the landscape and the sky. During daytime scenes, with the main lights full on, the backlights will not be apparent. As dusk approaches, and the main lights are dimmed, the sky will stay lit and silhouette the mountains. I have tried the lighting scheme on a mock-up and found the effect to be very realistic.

The backdrop can be attached directly to a nearby wall or supported by a separate structure. I found that 1 x 2 uprights attached to the rear of the benchwork are sufficient to support the backdrop. The 1″ side should face the backdrop. On straight sections, space the uprights at 16- to 24-inch increments if you're using sheet metal.

Since I chose to split my landscape and sky, separate supports were required for each. The sky backdrop was attached directly to the partition behind the layout. The landscape backdrop was supported by uprights. See fig. 2. [Figure 3 shows typical one-piece backdrop construction. — Ed.] The sky section extended from the ceiling down to about 62″ above the floor. The landscape part, which eventually had a profiled skyline (fig. 4), started several inches above the benchwork and rose to a height of 79″ above the floor, at the peak of the highest mountain.

There are several different types of materials that could be used as backdrop surfaces. Each has advantages and disadvantages. I tried three kinds: plasterboard, Masonite, and galvanized sheet metal.

I used ⅜″-thick plasterboard for straight sections of the sky backdrop and attached it directly to the partition with serrated wallboard nails. It is the least expensive, but also the heaviest and most easily damaged of the three materials. The big disadvantage is that it cannot be bent around corners.

I tried ¼″-thick Masonite for the first section of landscape I painted, although ⅛″-thick Masonite would have worked just as well. I attached it using countersunk wood screws. Masonite is an excellent material for backdrops. In ⅛″ thickness it can be used for moderately curved corners. Like plasterboard it comes in 4 x 8-foot panels. The tempered variety is the best. Install it with the smooth side out. It generally costs slightly more than plasterboard.

I first used galvanized sheet metal flashing for the curved sections of the sky backdrop. Its use was prompted by a planned 12″ radius for the teardrop curve at the end of the double-sided partition. This appeared to be too tight a curve for the Masonite. The sheet metal worked so well I used it to form the 90 degree corners as well. The material is very thin and was easily blended into the flat sections of the backdrop. I attached it to the vertical uprights with one countersunk wood screw at the top (be careful, the material is very thin) and a roundhead screw at the bottom.

After completely installing the sky backdrop, I realized that with the exception of the nearly completed and painted front

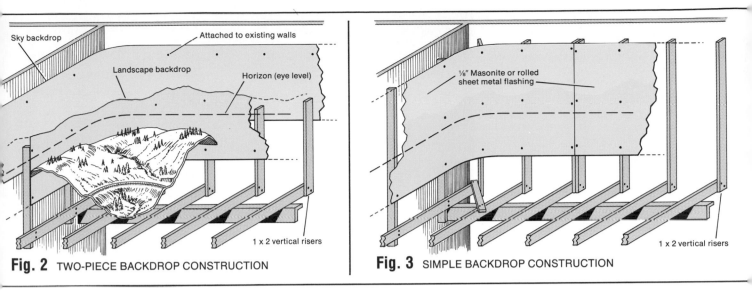

Fig. 2 TWO-PIECE BACKDROP CONSTRUCTION

Labels in Fig. 2: Sky backdrop; Attached to existing walls; Landscape backdrop; Horizon (eye level); 1 x 2 vertical risers

Fig. 3 SIMPLE BACKDROP CONSTRUCTION

Labels in Fig. 3: ⅛″ Masonite or rolled sheet metal flashing; 1 x 2 vertical risers

landscape section, the sheet metal curves covered most of the backdrop, and only a few feet of the plasterboard showed. In constructing the remainder of the landscape backdrop, I used a continuous piece of 20″-wide sheet metal flashing, which worked extremely well. It's strong, can be easily curved around corners, and requires no vertical joints. The best part is that it can be salvaged in one piece if the layout is dismantled.

Galvanized sheet metal flashing is commonly available in 50-foot rolls of 14″, 20″, and 28″ widths. It is slightly more than twice as expensive as tempered Masonite based on a sheet of Masonite yielding 16 linear feet of backdrop. You can buy it in cut lengths, but at a premium rate.

Aluminum flashing would also work, but it is more flexible and easily dented. The cost is comparable.

Regardless of the material used for the backdrop, vertical joints and screw or nail heads should be covered. Spackle or joint cement works well for all three materials. Paper tape used with joint cement helps to reinforce vertical butt joints. Before applying anything to the sheet metal, lightly sand the surface and wash it with detergent. This provides a clean rough surface for the spackle or cement. In more than 3 years I have had no problem with cracks or with pieces coming off the sheet metal or the other materials. After applying the compound, sand it smooth. Then apply two coats of white latex primer sealer to prepare the backdrop for painting.

SELECTING THE SCENE

Deciding what you are going to paint can be one of the most enjoyable parts of the project. Consider scenes that will blend in with your planned three-dimensional scenery and have the same geological character. The choices are virtually unlimited. I have found that by poring over different photographs and slides not only do I find some good candidates for the backdrop, but I can also get many new ideas for my three-dimensional scenery.

I am not very good at painting from mental images. I've found that using photographic aids is a tremendous help in creating a realistic and believable end result. If your choice of scenes is made carefully, keeping in mind several technical points I will discuss shortly, you will be relieved of many of the difficult aspects of backdrop painting. All you have to do is take your time and copy the photos.

Matching the horizons in the photos to the horizon on the backdrop is an important step. Given an average layout height of between 36″ and 48″ and an average eye level of 65″, it is clear that unless you are planning very tall mountains most of the scene will be below the horizon. In reviewing photos look for those in which about three quarters of the scene is below the horizon. If it appears that using the camera was pointed up, as in a closeup picture of a tall building, the horizon will be low or even out of the picture, and only the extremely low parts will be usable. Similarly, pictures of a valley taken from a mountaintop bias the horizon the other way, and the lower parts would be wasted. The best shots will have

a level, or slightly downward, camera angle and will have been taken from a vantage point where the photographer is slightly elevated.

Keeping track of perspective is another consideration. If you look down a long, straight stretch of track, you will observe that the rails, the telegraph lines, and everything else that parallels the track converges at a point in the distance. The convergence effect is called "perspective," and the spot where the lines join is what artists call the "vanishing point." Because of this, the way a scene looks depends on where you are standing. If you paint a scene where the perspective is very noticeable, it will look great from one spot but out of place from other viewing points.

Buildings or structures composed of straight lines tend to show perspective more than landscape. You can minimize the perspective on buildings by painting only the side that faces you. Another solution is to limit the viewing angles of the scene by framing it with three dimensional structures or trees so it will be seen only from a good angle.

Be on the lookout for shadows, and make sure their direction is the same from scene to scene and corresponds with the shadows cast by your structures and three-dimensional scenery. Some of the books and articles I have read say to avoid shadows in painted backdrops. I disagree. I think that painted shadows can help to give shape and contour to hills and ridges. The rugged appearance of most rock formations is enhanced by shadows.

There are many good sources of pictures for backdrop material: your own photographs or slides, postcards, books, and magazines such as *National Geographic* and *Arizona Highways*.

If you can find the right ones, slides are the best photographic medium for evaluating and painting a scene. In selecting the slides to use for continuing the already painted Mount Blanca section, I set up the projector across the room and aimed it at the blank backdrop where the scene would go. With just enough room light to see the features of the adjacent painted backdrop, I reviewed about 150 slides.

When I came upon a slide that provided a general match, I experimented by positioning the image in different relationships with respect to the painted scene. It turned out very much like testing the fit of a piece of jigsaw puzzle. Those matching the best appeared to lock in at the right position. Sometimes that resulted in a bit of overlap, and other times a gap was left. The technique is not limited to the projection of one slide. I have tried two and three projectors simultaneously with good results.

PREMIXING PAINTS

Here is a list of materials I used in painting my backdrop:
- Latex wall paint
- Tubes of acrylic colors
- Cups of the resulting mixtures
- Color charts used in mixing
- A half dozen good quality brushes.

Fig. 4. Right. The landscaped portion of the backdrop has a profiled skyline. The backdrop begins a few inches above the benchwork and extends to 79″ above the floor. After trying several materials, the author concluded that galvanized sheet metal was best for his sharply curved backdrop.

Fig. 5. Below. The author advises that each mix be labeled. You should also keep a rough record of each mix by dabbing a swatch on a chunk of cardboard and noting the mixture next to it as he has done on the cardboard shown here on the right.

Acrylic colors mixed with latex wall paint works well. Both are water-soluble and are completely compatible. Since latex paint is an increasingly popular base material for covering plaster scenery, its choice as the paint for your backdrop offers the additional advantage of requiring only one type of paint for all scenery projects and the ability to obtain a good color match between your three-dimensional scenery and backdrop.

I premix basic colors before starting to paint. This assures good color continuity and eliminates the patchwork effect that occurs when a large area is painted by mixing little puddles of colors.

In painting both the Mount Blanca and Red Mountain sections, I used four groups of premixed colors: tans, grays, reds, and greens. For each color I have a dark mix, a medium mix, and a light mix. The tans and grays and reds were used for both rocks and exposed earth. The lighter mixes were used in areas exposed to the sun, while the darker mixes were used in shaded sections. The greens were used for grass and trees, and included in addition to dark, medium, and light shades of green, was a light straw color to simulate dry grass. The two darkest green shades were used for the pine trees.

The basic colors in each group are a matter of personal taste. Your choice may be based on the colors of the chosen scene, your existing three-dimensional scenery, or perhaps the colors that dominate the area you are modeling. In blending

Fig. 6. The author used Wards "Tahoe" blue latex paint for the sky backdrop. **Fig. 7.** This slide of a Colorado mountain was projected and copied.

colors it is best to stay with simple mixes since you will probably want to make up another batch at a later time. Avoid developing formulas requiring "a pinch of this" and "a little bit of that." They are very difficult to reproduce. Excluding the white latex base and black acrylic, I used a maximum of three mixes in each group.

Start with the lightest color in each group. Put a quarter of a cup of latex ceiling white in a container. I use disposable plastic cups and plastic wrap over the top with a rubber band for a seal. Assuming that you mix about 16 colors, a quarter cup per mix will provide enough paint for a backdrop 2 feet high by 16 feet long. Add small, measured amounts of the dominant color. I measure the length in inches of the color extruded from the tube. Mix it up and paint a dab on the cardboard. Let it dry and observe the results. Keep adding, mixing, and checking until you reach the right approximate color. Mix the secondary colors, repeating the routine. Be careful when adding dark colors such as black. A little bit goes a long way. If you go way over when adding a darker color, it's often better to throw out the mix and start over since it will take a large amount of light paint to rebalance the mix.

To make the next darker mix in a color group, repeat the previous formula, adding more of the dominant colors. Again finish it off with the secondary colors. To prepare the darkest shade mix, add still more of the dominant color and a little black. The black will cause the mix to become grayer.

It is advisable to keep a rough record of colors and quantities as you try different mixes. This is easily done by dabbing a sample of each stage of the mix on a piece of cardboard and jotting down what you have added from the last step. See fig. 5. It is a convenient way to judge your progress and, if necessary, will allow you to retrace your steps. Be sure to let the paint dry for a minute or two before making any critical judgments. The colors change slightly as they dry. A written record and sample of each final paint mix should be made for future reference.

PAINTING THE BACKDROP

This is perhaps the most difficult aspect to describe. Because it is creative there are many approaches that lead to satisfactory results. I will describe one that works for me.

I use a three-step procedure. I do them sequentially, finishing one before proceeding to the next.

Step 1. Sketch the overall scene and paint each main area with its single most dominant color. Do not add any details.

Step 2. Sketch in lesser features. Paint in variations in intensity (light-dark) for shaded areas and changes in color. Avoid all but the largest details. Do not add trees or other "see through" objects.

Step 3. Fill in the details such as trees, rocks, roads, and distant structures to complete the scene.

Each step has a different objective. The first is to provide the basic forms and colors — get it up on the backdrop. Shaping the terrain and blending the colors are the aims of step 2. They should give the scene depth and dimension. Step 3 brings the scene into focus and gives it life. How far you go with these steps determines how detailed the backdrop will be. For example, step 1 alone will provide a basic background which may be just what you want. Others may want more detail and will continue into steps 2 and 3.

Paint the sky first. I use store-mixed latex. The right shade will probably be darker than you think it should be. Very light blues tend to wash out in photos. I used Wards "Tahoe" blue (187-B-3-71). Paint the backdrop blue from the top to slightly below the horizon. See fig. 6. As the sky approaches the horizon it becomes whiter. To achieve this effect, mix in progressively greater amounts of white. It is not necessary to have a perfectly smooth gradation from the dark blue at the top to the light at the horizon. A slight streakiness is quite acceptable because it suggests distant clouds.

Believable clouds are difficult to brush paint. There will be more clouds near the horizon because you are looking through more air. They will present a side view. Clouds higher in the sky will show more of their underside.

Overall scene. Now we're ready to paint the landscape. The first step is to make a rough sketch of the scene. I use a lead pencil. Don't use pens because the ink may bleed through. If you are working from a photograph, take time to make sure the proportions are correct and the horizons match. If working from a slide (fig. 7), project it on the backdrop and position the image, making sure it is level and the horizons are matched. Turn on enough room light so you can see the backdrop as you make the sketch as shown in fig. 8. Keep it simple, showing the skyline, major ridges, roads, rivers, borderlines separating woods and field, and outlines of objects like large rock formations and buildings. Also sketch in large shaded areas.

If you have chosen to separate the landscape backdrop from the sky backdrop, now is the time to trim the excess material from above the skyline.

Look for principal color areas in the slide or photo. In my backdrops this consisted of gray (with some tans and reds for the mountain peaks and rock formations), tan for the lower dirt slopes and other barren areas, and grass green for the meadows and forest areas. Although I left my trees until later, it would be acceptable to cover large areas of forest with its own color.

I used the middle shade in each of the color groups for the sunny areas and the darkest for the major shaded areas for this step.

The use of slides became advantageous at this point. While the sketch is gradually obscured as you paint, the slide image remains. You can paint or retrace the sketch directly from the image. During the early stages I often found it convenient to work directly from a slide image, although I would still recommend a rough sketch.

Fig. 8. In step 1 the author made a pencil sketch of the projected scene.   This is how the basic mountain backdrop painting looked at the end of step 1.

Fig. 8. These four photos show progress made during step 2. **Left.** Variations of gray and some browns are added and then **(above)** more light grays.

Refinement. During step 2 I try to refine the painting. At first the combined image became increasingly confusing, particularly where there were trees. The problem was overcome by the following four steps:

Step a. Trace a small area from the slide image.

Step b. Shut off the slide projector and paint from the sketch.

Step c. Turn on the projector and examine the match.

Step d. Repeat steps b and c until satisfied.

If you are working from a photograph, resketch any lines painted over and refine the scene to show all features which define the shape of the terrain. In doing step 2, I work on relatively small areas, going from background to foreground. My step 2 progress on this mountain scene is illustrated in fig. 9. Study the variations in contour and color. Observe where the ground is shaded and whether the transition from light to dark is gradual or abrupt.

Remember, the darkest mix should be used for the shadows while the medium shade is used in the sunny areas. Except for shadows cast by other objects, the nature of the transition is a visual key to the shape of the ground. A sharp transition indicates an edge. This can be used to show different sides of a building or, perhaps, a rocky ridge. There is also a sharp transition between the ridge line of a smooth hill and the distant scenery that it overlaps, but this has nothing to do with its shape.

On the other hand, if you can see both sides of a smooth rolling hill, there is a gradual change from its sunny side to its dark side. This is achieved by putting a dab of light paint on the sunny side near the transition and, likewise, a dab of dark paint on the other side. Before either has a chance to dry, blend them together by brushing back and forth. The further you brush, the larger the transition and the more gentle the curve of the hillside. It is difficult to describe, but easy to do. Experiment on a piece of cardboard. You will get the hang of it quickly.

Shadows produce interesting effects. I think they give a scene added dimension. Observe the scene you are working from and define the borderlines of shadows not covered in the first step. Their shapes and lengths will vary with the surfaces upon which they are cast and the angle of the scene, which needs to be established quite early.

At the same time you are developing the shape of the terrain by regulating the light-dark transitions, add the variations in color that you observe in the scene. This is also done by brushing dabs of different colors together. One dab should be the dominant color of the area while the other is the color of the desired variation, either from another color group or from very small amounts out of a tube.

Finally, use the lightest colors for highlighting the sunny areas. Check your slide or picture and try to hit only the brightest spots. Highlighting is very satisfying. It is like clearing away a heavy layer of clouds on a dark day. At the

same time you are doing the highlighting use a little bit of the medium mixes to moderate the shaded areas.

Final detailing. The last step is to add the details. In the scenes I painted, these consisted of rocks, trees, and several distant roads and mine structures. I will describe the technique I used for trees and rocks. Before you start, make sure you are satisfied with the shape and color of the terrain. Blending paints in an area is difficult once you've speckled it with details.

The trees in my scenes are spruce and pine. They appear in various size groups from patches of heavy forest to small clumps and individual trees. See fig. 10. They all have a very slender conical shape. To paint them, use the darkest and middle shades of greens. For large patches that completely cover an area, sketch in the outer boundaries and paint the area solid using the darkest mix. Remember that the top edges will have an irregular, sawtooth appearance. Then use the middle shade to highlight the sunny side of individual trees in the forest. Do not highlight trees completely in the shade. In clumps of only a few trees, the shapes of individual trees become important. Likewise trees in the foreground should receive more attention than background trees. Study the photos or slides you are working from.

Deciduous, or leaf-bearing trees, have different shapes than pine trees and require a little different technique. For individual trees, dab on splotches of the darkest shade, forming the basic outline of the tree. In making each splotch try to gently stab at the surface of the backdrop, causing the bristles

Fig. 9. These photos illustrate step 3. First distance trees are painted.

Above. The contour of the foothills has been refined. **Right.** Further softening and highlighting of the foothills greatly improves the appearance.

to spread out in all directions. If you wipe off some of the paint before you start each brushful, the splotches will have an open, ragged appearance, looking more like the texture of a tree. Add splotches of the middle shade and finally the lightest mix, working your way to the sunny side of the tree. Different types of trees can be made by varying colors and shapes. Add the trunk and major branches using medium and dark grays and tans. Adding a few splotches of green after painting the branches places them in, rather than on, the leaves.

Paint large areas of deciduous trees in the same way as you would the pines. Cover the areas initially with the darkest mix, providing an irregular profile at the top by using the splotch technique. Fill in the center area with the lighter shades, and paint trunks and branches only for the trees in front; none if the trees are in the distance.

Most trees in a forest are about the same height. By making the trees in the foreground larger than those in the background you can increase the illusion of distance. This is particularly effective in areas where there are no other features to show distance. Small clumps of individual trees work best for this purpose.

Rock formations are easy to paint. Outline the formation and paint it solid using the middle shade of the rock colors. Carefully observe the details of the formation in the picture. Note the general shape of the individual rocks that make it up. Younger rocks, as in the Rocky Mountains, are jagged and angular. Rocks from older mountains such as the Alleghenies

often have rounded edges. Sedimentary rocks show a strong layered effect.

Look for major shaded surfaces, cracks and fissures. Paint these with the darkest mix. I generally fill in lesser surfaces and cracks without trying to follow the picture. The object is to establish the same texture; in practice it is much like doodling.

Now refer back to the picture and look for the very bright surfaces. Paint these using the lightest mix.

Note how the formation blends into the surrounding terrain. Most large formations are surrounded by smaller rocky areas and loose rock that has broken off. Remember, loose chunks generally come to rest on larger, more stable surfaces. Also, the longer they have been there the more imbedded they will appear.

You can paint individual rocks in the foreground using a scaled-down version of the techniques just described. Just apply paint spots using the middle shades. If enough of the rock is exposed to give it a shaded area, dab on a little of the darkest mix. Sometimes I use highlighting, sometimes not. Often, smaller foreground rocks are just spots of the middle shade. Paint fewer rocks and make them smaller as you recede into the distance.

If you have read this entire article you have at least a flicker of interest in trying to paint a backdrop. So get out some photos of your favorite scenes that might just fit in over behind the yard, or perhaps out at the junction, and get painting. I think you'll surprise yourself. ⌗

Above. Next, the tops of a row of deciduous trees are painted. **Right.** Finally, the trunks of the larger foreground trees and other details are added.

Structures as background scenery

Who says you can't use N scale buildings on an HO layout?

BY DAVE FRARY
PHOTOS BY THE AUTHOR

THIS IS GOING TO SOUND like heresy to a lot of dedicated structure builders, but on my HOn2½ Carrabassett & Dead River RR a lot of the buildings aren't HO scale structures at all. Some are N scale, and some are even smaller. These buildings serve in the background and are more part of the scenery than models in their own right. They have only two or three sides, and I build and paint them using scenery techniques. Building such background buildings is fast and easy, and I'll show you how.

BUT FIRST, A SMATTERING OF THEORY

The further we are from objects on the railroad, the less detailed they need to be. Also, distant objects can be made smaller than scale to make them appear even further away.

For example, foreground trees can be built with realistic colors, shapes, and detailed leaf textures, but middle-distance trees (2 or 3 feet from the front edge of the layout) need only be correctly shaped, colored, and textured, as well as slightly smaller. Trees in the background can be simply groups of smaller, textured shapes. Anyone viewing these middle distance and background trees subconsciously accepts them as having the same details and scale fidelity as those up front.

In the same way, background buildings can be undersize caricatures of buildings — with the correct shape, color, and some of the surface texture, but without most of the detail. So, I use full-scale HO structures in the foreground and large N scale structures in the middle distance. Near the background I use parts of small N scale structures and smaller-scale scratchbuilt buildings. Many of these are just hand-colored structures made with a copy machine, as shown in fig. 1.

COPY MACHINE STRUCTURES

I start by selecting plans published in model railroad magazines, architectural journals, and library books. Choosing several likely buildings at a time saves trips to the copier.

First, I reduce the plan to about N scale, although scale is not critical. What is important is getting the cleanest copy possible. Then I reduce this copy again until it looks small enough to fit its planned location. Incidentally, you can use the same building in several locations, provided you vary the sizes and the colors.

I glue the reduced copies to cardboard using spray glue or rubber cement, then color the structures with water colors, artist's magic markers, and colored pencils. (If you have total access to a plain-paper copier you may want to try copying the plans onto colored paper. I like Canary Yellow and Pastel Blue.) To finish these paper buildings I blacken all the windows and add shadows under the overhangs, such as the eaves or window sills.

I cut out the buildings with a sharp hobby knife and assemble the parts with white glue. I might add some simple details, and then I dust the structure with pastel chalks to kill any paper shine.

OTHER BACKGROUND BUILDINGS

Even a small N scale plastic structure provides the raw material for several different background models, as shown in fig. 2. To disguise the origins of your buildings, you'll want to interchange parts from several kits, mixing the walls, roofs, and trim.

Besides using kit parts, I also scratch-build walls from brick-, stone-, or block-textured building papers and plastic sheet glued over heavy cardboard. (There are many types and textures of building papers shown in Walthers' catalog. I use those made by Faller, SS Ltd., and Kibri). To make a building look different when seen from various places on the layout, you can paint one wall to represent weathered wood and glue brick or stone paper to another.

You don't need to spend time cutting openings for doors and windows in these background buildings. After some simple preparation I just glue the door and window castings right on the walls. First I glue acetate to the rear of the painted window castings, then I paint the back side (the surface that will go against the wall) with Polly S paint to add both curtains and black emptiness. When the paint is dry I glue the window onto the wall. Any extra thickness won't be noticed because the model is so far from the viewer. If a particular door or window should look too thick, I paint the frame a dark color to minimize its size.

Freight doors can be glued on the building walls anywhere there is room for them. If doors are overly thick, I sand them thinner before gluing them on. Porches, sheds, shutters, etc., can be cut from wood blocks and strips, painted, and added to the wall sections. A little trimming with a hobby knife can transform unlikely plastic parts into useful details.

THE ALL-IMPORTANT ROOF

The roof is a prominent part of most background buildings, and it's usually seen first. I start with wood shingle, slate, and asphalt texture papers from Rix and Kibri. Over this plain paper or plastic roof I add scratchbuilt details or leftover items from other modeling projects.

You can make stovepipes from wire and tubing, and brick chimneys from blocks of wood with building paper glued around them. Fans, ventilators, and skylights are stolen from plastic kits. I paint and weather such details before adding them to the roof, then dust the entire roof with pastel chalks to weather the surfaces and tone down the colors.

PAINTING TECHNIQUES

Correct painting is important to make

Fig. 1. Left. There's less to some structures on Dave Frary's layout than meets the eye. The background buildings on the hillside here add tremendous depth and interest to the scene. Viewed up close (above) they're simple structures, smaller than N scale, and made by gluing copy machine copies to cardboard.

Fig. 2. Left. Here's another example of how undersized background buildings can add depth to the scene. The cream-colored grain elevator, distant left, was made from a Quality Craft N scale kit. The row of stores (shown closer above) was built from Magnuson N scale kits. Angling the corners on one end adds interest. The church and other distant structures are buildings — or only pieces of buildings — constructed from inexpensive N scale plastic kits.

these structures look far away. I paint mid-distance buildings with colors which are muted by mixing about 20 percent earth color or gray with them. I increase the amount of gray or earth color to about 40 percent for distant structures.

To bring out the surface detail on the background structures, I use a three-step process. First, the complete building is painted with grayed colors. After this dries, I turn the building upside down and flow a black oil wash onto all the surfaces.

I make this wash by mixing a little (¼ tsp.) lamp black with a 5-ounce baby food jar of mineral spirits (cheap paint thinner). After the thinner dries it leaves a 'shadow' of lampblack under all the surface texture.

Next I highlight the raised surfaces of the building by drybrushing them with Polly S Reefer White. To do this use an old stiff brush to lift a little paint from the jar, then stroke most of the paint from the brush onto a piece of waxed paper. Keep stroking until the paint thickens and starts to dry. To see if the brush has the right amount of paint on it, stroke it softly across the palm of your hand — it will leave a little wisp of white when it's ready for drybrushing.

Drag the brush over the raised parts of the structure, starting at the roof top and working down. The idea is to leave a trace of white on the raised edges. This highlights and shows off the detail that would normally be lost due to the distance.

If still more accent is needed, or if I have gone too far with the drybrushing, I can correct or add to my coloring by weathering the building with pastel chalks. I use them to dull any plastic shine, to add black shadows under roof eaves and on the far side of walls, and to give the building a bluish, hazy look.

INSTALLING BACKGROUND BUILDINGS

Background structures like the hilltop hotel shown in fig. 3 can be placed during scenery construction or years later. I usually build wood foundations in places where I expect to locate buildings, covering them with a brick or stone texture paper, leveling them, and gluing them in place. I bring the scenery up to the foundations with ground foam and bits of lichen or other greenery. Small trees and larger clumps of lichen can be used to hide any irregularities between the foundation and the ground contour.

I set newly constructed background buildings on these foundations for evaluation; often a structure built for one location looks even better someplace else. As a result, I build most of my small-scale buildings without a specific location in mind, then move them around to find a pleasing spot. The buildings are never glued in place, so it's easy to change the look of the layout.

TAILORING BACKGROUND BUILDINGS TO YOUR LAYOUT

When a background building must fit a specific spot, cut a cardboard base to fit the location, then build a cardboard mock-up of the structure to fit the base. Sometimes I try several different mock-ups on the base to find the best shape and size. Remember, walls and corners need not be square, and background buildings that will be viewed from more than one angle can have walls with different textures for each angle. If it looks good, use it.

Once you have a mock-up that you like, take it to the workbench, disassemble it, and use the cardboard parts as templates to build the permanent building.

These small background structures are fun to build, require very little time and money, and create an illusion of depth on the layout. Best of all, they blend in so naturally they become part of the scenery. ✿

Fig. 3. Left. The imposing resort hotel on the hill is in fact a simple background structure made from an N scale Magnuson Models kit. The roof is just painted cardboard, and the porch is also cardboard. The smaller shot above, taken from an angle where the building is never viewed normally, shows how basic the model and its site really are. The hotel is not glued down and could be moved to another location.

The ultimate condensation

A model industry that isn't there

BY G. WARREN REED

EXPLOSIVES factories are among the most difficult large industries to condense to reasonable model proportions. That's because, like the two large explosives plants near Birmingham, Alabama., they usually have several buildings spread over a large area to reduce damage and injuries in accidents.

I took a closer look at one plant served by a railroad and found that I really wasn't seeing very much. The railroad branch passes the plant's front gate and continues down one boundary. The only buildings at the gate are a security building and a small office. From the track I couldn't see anything else but a fence, as vegetation and small hills screen the factory buildings.

Even the railroad spur into the plant offers no view of the facilities. A single track leaves the branch, curves through some trees, and disappears from sight. The only evidence of the explosives factory is the warning signs and the fence. A cut of cars sitting just inside the plant boundary simply appears to be parked out in the woods.

Applying John Armstrong's principle of suggestive omission, a modeler can create a major industry for his railroad with a minimum of space and effort. The sprawling explosives plant needn't be modeled at all, merely suggested by a spur passing through a fence and disappearing behind wooded hills, with signs for identification.

The prototype I visited had only small signs which would almost disappear if reduced to scale. I made larger signs for my layout from Plastruct shapes and used scale 10″ black dry-transfer lettering on a yellow-painted background for visibility. Placing the signs in the scenery where the spur leaves the branch and planting some chain link fence are the minimum requirements for this maximum condensation.

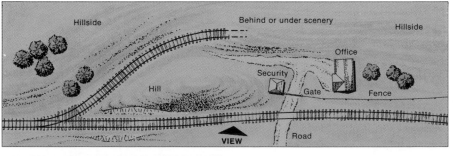

VERSION WITH OFFICE AND FRONT GATE

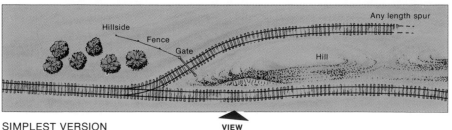

SIMPLEST VERSION

USEFUL ADDRESSES

Your local hobby shop is always the best place to look
for scenery products, tools, and materials, but here
are current addresses for the manufacturers of some
of the special items mentioned in this book

A. M. S. I.
115-B Bellam Blvd., P. O. Box 3497
San Rafael, CA 94912

Bachmann
1400 East Erie Avenue.
Philadelphia, PA 19124

Dover Publications
180 Varick Street
New York, NY 10014

Edmund Scientific Co.
101 East Glouster Pike
Barrington, NJ 08007

Enviro Tex
P. O. Box 365
Fields Landing, CA 95537

Floquil-Polly S Color Corp.
Route 30 North
Amsterdam, NY 12010

I. H. C. (formerly A. H. M.)
350 East Tioga Street
Philadelphia, PA 19134

Percy Harms Corp.
P. O. Box 156
Wheeling, IL 60090

Precision Scale Co.
1120-A Gum Avenue
Woodland, CA 95695

Vintage Reproductions
2606 Flintridge Drive
Colorado Springs, CO 80918

**V. L. S. Warwinds
International**
West Port Industrial Park
804 Fee Fee Road
Maryland Heights, MO 63043

William K. Walthers
5601 West Florist Avenue.
Milwaukee, WI 53218

Woodland Scenics
P. O. Box 98
Linn Creek, MO 65052

INDEX